*

Why Putting Your Kids First Is the **Last Thing** You Should Do

*

The Happiest Mommy You Know

Genevieve Shaw Brown

TOUCHSTONE BOOKS

New York   London   Toronto   Sydney   New Delhi

Certain names and identifying characteristics have been changed.

Touchstone
An Imprint of Simon & Schuster, Inc.
1230 Avenue of the Americas
New York, NY 10020

First Touchstone trade paperback edition October 2017

TOUCHSTONE and colophon are registered trademarks
of Simon & Schuster, Inc.

For information about special discounts for bulk purchases,
please contact Simon & Schuster Special Sales at 1-866-506-1949
or business@simonandschuster.com.

The Simon & Schuster Speakers Bureau can bring authors to your live event.
For more information or to book an event contact the Simon & Schuster Speakers
Bureau at 866-248-3049 or visit our website at www.simonspeakers.com.

Interior design by Kyle Kabel

Photos courtesy of the author

Manufactured in the United States of America

10 9 8 7 6 5 4 3 2 1

The Library of Congress has cataloged the hardcover edition as follows:

Names: Brown, Genevieve Shaw, author.
Title: The happiest mommy you know : why putting your kids first is the last thing
you should do / Genevieve Shaw Brown.
Description: New York : Touchstone Books, [2017] | Includes index.
Identifiers: LCCN 2016021620 (print) | LCCN 2016033803 (ebook)
Subjects: LCSH: Motherhood. | Mothers. | Well-being.
Classification: LCC HQ759 .B75944 2017 (print) | LCC HQ759 (ebook) |
DDC 306.874/3—dc23
LC record available at https://lccn.loc.gov/2016021620

ISBN 978-1-5011-3578-1
ISBN 978-1-5011-3579-8 (pbk)
ISBN 978-1-5011-3583-5 (ebook)

For Ryan, Addie, Will, and Luke—my happily ever after.

Contents

Introduction

Why Putting Yourself First (Sometimes) Is Actually the Best Thing You Can Do for Your Kids

You know the drill, moms. We make perfectly frosted cupcakes for our kid's classroom, then scarf one down on the way to school because we forgot to eat breakfast ourselves. Our children are always beautifully decked out in coordinated clothes, while we live in black workout pants. We take our little ones to the doctor every time they have the sniffles, but we haven't scheduled a checkup in two years.

Sound familiar? Yeah, to me as well. Heck, this was me . . . until recently. I'm the one who was so intent on doing this mom thing "right" that I began to lose sight of everything that made me, me.

But I'll tell you who I am these days. I'm the mom who finally managed to lose those last pounds of pregnancy weight, after years of trying and failing. I'm the one who goes on vacation with my husband, sans kids. I'm the one who found time to meet up with my best friend for a drink last week.

And you know what? I'm a lot happier—and a better mom—for it. Being a better mother, after all, was the goal all along.

The "secret" is rather simple. I stopped putting my kids first every second of every day. I looked at how well I treated them (and how poorly I treated myself). And I wondered, what would happen if I lavished myself with the same kind of love and care that I give to them?

Does that sound like sacrilege? I used to think so, too.

It was a long road to get here. There were some bumps and missteps along the way. A few surprises, too! But today life is a lot saner, a lot smoother, and a lot, yes, happier now that I've learned one simple secret: Treat yourself as well as you treat your kids.

That's it.

I'm not telling you to neglect your kids. Instead, think about yourself for a change. Prioritize your own needs—eating well, getting enough sleep, spending time with your partner and your friends, even starting a new hobby. Be a little (gasp!) selfish, in the name of ultimately being a better mom. For once, treat yourself with the same care and love you give to your kids every day. That's what I learned how to do (in a long, painful, sometimes funny process, which I'll outline for you in this book). It wasn't always pretty, but it sure has yielded great rewards since I started this little experiment with my own family.

Oh yeah, family. Because that's what it's all about, right? Let me get this out of the way right now: I love my kids more than anything in the world, rivaled perhaps only by the adoration I feel for my husband. We all love our families and want to do everything for them. We cook them nutritious meals. We set up carefully curated playdates and wonderfully diverse extracurricular activities. We dress them in crisp, carefully laundered, beautifully made outfits. We go to extraordinary measures to be sure they get a good night's sleep.

And that's all wonderful! Good for us. Pats on the back all around. But here's the thing: when your kid is eating free-range organic food and you're scarfing down fast food in the car, or your child is on the second playdate of the weekend and you haven't seen your best friend for two months, something is dangerously out of whack. We need to take back some of our power, some of our agency, some of our time, and stop putting our loved ones' needs before ours at every opportunity.

Moms, listen to this: putting your kids first is the *last* thing you should do. Instead, try gifting yourself a little of the care, attention, and love you so generously give to your family every day. Read on, and I'll tell you why . . . and how this revolutionary philosophy worked wonders on my health, my marriage, my friendships, my happiness—and most importantly, ultimately made me a better mom.

I've started listening to what I need again. I'm here to tell you, the secret to being the Happiest Mommy You Know (or even just, you know, *happier*) isn't perfection. Far from it. It's a surprisingly simple, slightly counterintuitive tip I learned the hard way.

Putting yourself first sometimes is actually the best thing you can do for your kids.

I did it. I'll show you how. You can do it, too.

Chapter 1

Holy Crap, I Eat Like Crap

Feed Yourself as You (Want to) Feed Your Kids

It was about 5 a.m. My husband, three-year-old daughter, and fourteen-month-old son were still fast asleep in our New York City apartment. I had risen earlier than they, as was the typical drill, to get myself ready for work. Part of that routine included preparing the food that the children would eat throughout the day, until I returned home in time to make them dinner that evening.

I didn't mind the early morning so much. Truth be told, I've never been one to sleep in. Even before kids, it wasn't uncommon for me to get up a little early to go for a run or enjoy a leisurely cup of coffee before heading off to work, though now that I was a mom those small luxuries were a thing of the distant past. So I wasn't exactly prepared for the new wake-up time that having kids imposed on my schedule. Six thirty, even six would be OK. But there's something ungodly about five.

At five in the morning, the light from the refrigerator is so bright, it feels like an interrogation.

Every. Single. Day.

It's not that my youngest, Will, woke up at five. But he is an early riser—almost always before six when he was younger—and so 5 a.m. became my wake-up time in order to do everything that needed to be done before going into full-fledged mommy duty. Which mostly consisted of meal prep—cooking the meals the kids would eat while I was at work, and then getting things ready for the dinner that would be served shortly after I arrived home in the evening.

The thought of me cooking—never mind cooking at 5 a.m., pajama clad and bleary eyed—would be laughable to most of my friends. One of my friends' favorite stories about me was when, already a fully grown adult with my own apartment, I had to ask what a ramekin was when a recipe I was attempting called for this particular piece of cookware. The Barefoot Contessa I'm not.

The truth is, it was only since having kids that I even gave a second thought to what I was eating. Up until my late twenties, I was always on the slim side, despite eating mostly crap. By *crap* I mean takeout most nights, few vegetables, and a preference for food dripping with cheese. (Yeah, I know—I hate the twentysomething me, too.) Despite a diet more suited to a sumo wrestler than a busy journalist, I was declared to be in perfect health by every doctor I ever had the infrequent occasion to visit.

Fast forward many years of marriage and one baby . . . then two . . . and I found myself in an average-to-most-but-borderline-unacceptable-by-New-York-City–standards body. Not that I was sweating it, *exactly*, but at some point after the birth of my second child I had a realization: *Holy crap. I eat like crap.*

The realization, however, did little to change my habits. Sure, I'd occasionally wake up on Monday and declare this to be the Week of Salads (only to have my resolution fizzle by the time I passed the latest tempting food truck parked outside my office on Tuesday at lunch). Mostly, I had no willpower when it came to what I considered my last remaining vice: food. And to tell you the truth, it didn't bother me that much. I had a slightly superior mind-set: because I didn't smoke, use drugs, drink to excess (and was, in most regards, a model citizen, ahem), I guess I believed that I deserved to eat what I wanted. Never mind that all that crap food was starting to make me feel like a crap person, something that would take me a long time to understand.

At the time Will began to eat solid foods, I became determined not to pass along my less-than-optimal approach to eating. You see, I was harboring a shameful secret. I'd already failed once. My three-year-old, Addie, was a picky eater. And judging by the Facebook groups of New York City moms I belonged to, having a three-year-old who ate little aside from fruit, yogurt, peanut butter sandwiches, and plain pasta was akin to child abuse.

I could not fail again.

I started reading a lot about proper nutrition for babies, scouring the Internet for baby-recipe inspiration. For guidance, I turned to sites such as Weelicious and Picky Palate, where I found a veritable wonderland of clever ways to hide vegetables in food or make it so adorable that my kids couldn't help but pop it in their mouths. Armed with ideas for Scrambled Egg and Broccoli Cups and Cauliflower Mashed "Potatoes," Mapo Tofu, and Sautéed Baby Bok Choy, I spent my early-morning hours stirring couscous on the stovetop, baking sweet potatoes in the oven, dicing up rotisserie chicken, and creating fruit and vegetable smoothies that tasted sweet enough from the fruit to be appealing but did not *completely* mask the vegetable taste (so as not to raise a child who did not welcome vegetables onto his plate at every meal). You know the drill.

It would be easy enough to lose oneself completely in the information, recipes, planning, apps, mommy groups, and more that are dedicated to kids' nutrition. But time is one thing I'm perennially short on: I have a full-time job at ABC News, where I am responsible for leading its online lifestyle coverage. It's a big job, one I worked for years to attain, and it keeps me pretty busy. Luckily, since I cover a fair amount of parenting topics in my reporting job, there's some overlap in the research I do for my kids and the background info I seek for my stories. (So if I got busted looking at Weelicious recipes at the office, it could easily be assumed it had something to do with an article I was researching.)

That morning, I arrived at my desk, worried about the possible long-term ramifications of Will's refusal to eat more than two bites of his eggs. *Was he getting enough protein? Toddlers really need protein, right?* In between scanning the lifestyle stories and pitches that might possibly make the day's list of coverage, I start googling.

Egg substitutes for kids who don't like eggs
Is dislike for eggs a sign of an egg allergy?
Alternative protein options for toddler breakfast
How to make your toddler eat eggs
This is silly, I tell myself. *Get a grip.* I try to put eggs out

of my mind, refocus my attention, and prepare to start my workday. But the worry about the eggs—*Maybe he was full by the time we got around to the eggs?*—nags at me as I try to focus on the task at hand: I am responsible for choosing, assigning, and crafting the ABC News lifestyle stories that everyone will be talking about tomorrow. This is a big job. I need to concentrate. And yet . . . eggs. *Mmmm . . .*

All this thinking about breakfast food caused me to glance at the clock, and I realized, it's 9:58. *I'm starving! Did I eat breakfast this morning?* Nope. There's not enough time to get to the ABC cafeteria—it closes at ten for breakfast—to get my own eggs. None of my coworkers seem to have this daily issue of not getting to the cafeteria on time to get their breakfast (then again, most of them don't have kids). As I looked around the newsroom, I found eggs galore, oatmeal, pancakes, and yogurt. Yogurt! I packed one this morning. I reach to my bag and . . . no yogurt. I left it on the counter in the kitchen.

Back to work, my stomach empty save the two cups of coffee and cup of water. *No matter . . . I'll wait for lunch.* And then by eleven thirty, when I was so hungry I could no longer think straight, I headed to the cafeteria (now reopened) and walked around aimlessly looking for something to eat. But time was ticking and the emails were coming in faster than I could answer them, so I headed to the shortest line I saw: comfort food.

Chicken nuggets. Mac and cheese. Mashed potatoes. *Looks like food kids would love,* I thought. *I guess that's why it's called comfort food. It reminds us of childhood.* I thought about Will, probably at this moment sitting down in his high chair, eating organic turkey meatballs filled with veggies, a small side of couscous, and some sliced fruit for dessert. *Lucky kid*, I thought, as I piled "comfort food" into a paper box to be weighed at the register. *Will comfort remind Will of his childhood? Ha! Probably not.*

I realize that I wish I could eat like Will. I wish someone would make me all that delicious, healthy food. I'd probably feel better *and* lose those last few pounds. I need a nutritionist. Someone who will plan my meals and balance out my protein-to-grain-to-carb intake. *Why don't I take better care of myself?*

The thoughts start spiraling: *You are so lazy. Why can't you just eat better? What is wrong with you? Look around! There's a reason the junk-food line is the shortest. This food stuff is terrible for you. If only I had something better.* And then it hit me. That delicious, healthy food I'd been up at five preparing for my kids? I had never once—until that moment—considered allowing myself to eat any of it.

Crazy, right?

I had been berating myself for my unhealthy eating habits, but my only solutions so far had been searching under the "healthy" tab on Seamless (so virtuous, I know) or looking for the best-worst option in a fast-food line. All the while, I had actually been *going* food shopping for healthy food, week after week, and then actually preparing it each day. Just not for myself. For my kids.

Every day, I was greeted with a refrigerator full of healthy food. Every day, I didn't eat it. And God help my husband if he touched it. *That food was for the baby.*

But why? Why wasn't I allowing myself to partake in this nutritious food? What would happen if I treated myself with the same love, care, and nurturing that I lavished on my children each day?

Does Good Parenting Always Mean Putting Our Kids First?

I know this question (as simple as it sounds) will be eerily familiar to other moms out there. Mothers today take an almost perverse pride in how much we do for our kids. One can see it in nearly every single modern-parenting debate. If you cosleep, it's because you can't stand to be away from your baby and don't care if your own sleep is interrupted as long as the little one is content. If you don't, it's because you want to foster your child's independence and bestow on her the path to a life of good sleeping habits.

If you work, it's because you want to show your kids what it means to be an independent woman who contributes financially to the family and has a life outside the home. If you stay at home, it's because you care more about your family than any job, and being with the children is your top priority.

Choices, sacrifices, and justifications to be sure, but any choice you make is always tinged with the underlying fear of messing everything up. And let's remember, all of it is done out of one singular feeling: total and unconditional love for your children.

Love for our offspring—that's what we as parents have in common, isn't it? But how does that love influence our happiness? Are we happier because we're parents? There are conflicting studies on this front. In 2013, a British study from Open University dubbed the "Enduring Love" project declared childless couples were happier than those with children. It reported that mothers are more negative about relationship quality, relationship with partner, relationship maintenance, and happiness with their relationship or partner than childless women are. There's also the oft-cited 2004 study, conducted by Nobel Prize–winner Dr. Daniel Kahneman, of 909 working Texas mothers that showed child care as ranking 16th of 19 in pleasurable activities. Child care came in behind other daily responsibilities including cooking, watching TV, and socializing with coworkers. Another study, "In Defense of Parenthood," published in 2013 in *Psychological Science*, shows men with children were happier than men without kids. But here's the kicker: having children did not make women any happier than their childless counterparts.

It's easy to jump to the conclusion that, at least for some parents, an overinvestment in our children is at least in part contributing to the seeming dissatisfaction. The logical conclusion might be to stop being so emotionally, physically, and financially invested in your children, and you'll find more time for you and, as a result, you'll be happier. But let me get this out of the way right upfront: I don't buy it.

On the contrary, my children have made me happier than I ever thought possible. There are moments I think my heart will actually explode with love for them. There are times when we stare into each other's eyes, and I actually feel like our hearts are speaking to each other. When they are not physically near me, my heart aches for them. Sometimes when I put them to bed at night, at the same time that I breathe a sigh of relief, the tears start falling because I'm so sad at the thought of another day of their precious, too-short childhood gone.

I know I'm not alone in these feelings. My circle of "mom friends" is wide—partly because of the flexibility afforded to me by my employer. I am a full-time working mother who also has the ability to attend baby music, gym, ballet and swimming classes, playgroups, school drop-off, playdates, and more. As a result, I am friendly with not only mothers whose circumstances are similar to my own but also with working moms who work long hours, stay-at-home moms with help and those without, moms with husbands who work late, and single moms going at it alone. I also have one child with special needs—my son, Will, has Down syndrome—and one without, and as such, I have a foot in each of those worlds, too.

Befriending mothers in various situations has given me firsthand knowledge that my passionate love for my kids is, well, pretty universal and not at all unique. It also assures me that I'm not alone in feeling overwhelmed to the point of near panic attacks by the massive responsibility of someone else's (in my case two other someone's) well-being. And then there's the guilt. It's all consuming and it's constant. Every bedtime story not read, every enrichment class not enrolled in, every vegetable on the toddler's plate that goes uneaten is a source of stress.

But the evidence is far from conclusive when it comes to declaring kids the source of unhappiness. That Open University study from 2013 that showed childless couples were happier than those with children? It also showed mothers were the happiest group of all. And a 2013 study, "Parents Reap What They Sow: Child-Centrism and Parental Well-Being," from *Social Psychological and Personality Science*, concluded that "contrary to popular belief, more child-centric parents reported deriving more happiness and meaning from parenthood." In other words, the tendency for parents to prioritize their children's well-being above their own wasn't necessarily a bad thing or, at the very least, it doesn't apply across the board.

This seems to be the camp I, and the women I know, fall into: a life that is both generally happy and child-centric, but coupled with feelings of self-doubt and a touch of longing for a life that is less anxiety-filled. In Jennifer Senior's bestselling book *All Joy and No Fun: The Paradox of Modern Parenthood*, she turned the tide of the parenting discussion by asking what effect children have on their parents. Until Senior's book, the exploration of the parent-child relationship had been nearly exclusively focused on what effect parents had on their kids. By observing and examining parent groups and specific families, Senior quite correctly concludes that having kids is always a game changer—for your marriage, your friendships, your professional life.

There's also the issue of categorization of parenting styles, which is a relatively new phenomenon. There's the helicopter mom who hovers too close; the Tiger mom who only accepts total and complete excellence; the attachment parent who responds immediately to every need of the child; the free-range parent who encourages independence from a young age. While each one has its passionate supporters and detractors, there's no doubt that each one has positive traits. After all, if you could raise your child to succeed academically while being independent yet simultaneously knowing he or she can call you and trust that you'll be there at a moment's notice, why wouldn't you? But with all the label-parenting comes the pressure as a mother to decide which camp you belong in, rather than to simply just . . . parent.

But no matter which parenting discipline you follow (even if you follow none at all), there's a common theme that seems to unite all of us: we are all determined to do whatever it takes to make our kids happy, healthy, to give them a leg up in the world. We're so hell-bent on this that we'll get up at 5 a.m. to cook their organic couscous. We'll schlep them to karate lessons on Saturday morning instead of going to the gym ourselves. We let them sleep in our beds (even if we're up tossing and turning all night). But with all this focusing on our child's wants and needs, where do *our* needs fit in? Are we dooming ourselves to a lifetime (well, maybe a decade or two) of skipped meals, missed workouts, and sleepless nights?

There's got to be a better way.

The Baby Diet

But back to my lunchtime cafeteria revelation. That fateful day—as hectic, harried, and hungry as it was—was not an aberration. It was the norm. I never ate breakfast. My days consisted of raiding the ABC News cafeteria for an early lunch, maybe wolfing down a snack in the afternoon, likely followed by standing in front of the refrigerator when I got home, looking for anything to tide me over until the inevitable take-out order once the kids were in bed.

And I wondered why I couldn't lose the last of that baby weight.

Research from the University of Michigan shows that mothers have a higher body-mass index than nonmothers and consume more calories in a day than childless women. The result? Parents are more apt to not take good care of their health at a time when they really need to be modeling healthy behavior for their children.

The answer to healthier eating suddenly seemed so obvious: If I could eat the same foods I was feeding my toddler—in effect, stop putting my own needs behind his—I would be well on my way to changing my abysmal eating habits. And at the same time, I'd be modeling better eating for Addie, my three-year-old picky eater. I would put myself on the baby's diet.

I started talking with New York–based nutritionist Nicolette Pace, who explained to me that babies have a natural rhythm when it comes to eating that we lose at some point as we grow.

"We need to look to our babies for the answers," she said. Pace points out that we used to be a 9-to-5 workday society. "Now," she said, "it's more like five to nine." If we follow our children's rhythms (not just in what they eat, but when and why), she says, we can get back to a schedule that will help our bodies find their optimal weight.

A lightbulb went off. That was it exactly: my day started at five with those fateful meal preparations. Then came two hours of child care before heading to my office for another eight. Then it was time to head home for another three hours of child care—dinner, bath, books, bed—before almost collapsing from physical, mental, and emotional exhaustion at 9 p.m. Five to nine. That was my day.

"We prioritize everything above eating," Pace said. "But our babies—if they're hungry, we'll move hell and high water to make sure they're fed."

As adults, she added, we rarely do the same for ourselves. I flash back to the scene in my kitchen on a typical morning. I'm hell-bent on preparing a healthy breakfast and making sure the kids eat it, because I believe—scratch that, I *know*—what they eat in the morning will set the tone for the rest of the day. I am so tied to this belief, in fact, that I try—and often fail, but do try—to have them eat their foods in a particular order.

So, if, for example, breakfast consists of fruit, yogurt, and a piece of toast with butter, I will do my best to serve it in that order, with the buttered toast coming last. I do it so they'll eat the healthier food while they're hungriest, and so that they won't fill up on the toast and leave the healthy stuff on the plate. I'm not sure if I read this somewhere or just made it up, but it's become gospel in my house: healthy foods first.

Clearly I have put thought into this.

Meanwhile, I rarely eat breakfast myself. That sinks in. I'm so concerned with what my kids are eating for breakfast so it will set the wheels in motion for a healthy day that I actually serve foods in a particular order. And I don't even bother putting one morsel in my own mouth.

Pace said not skipping meals is one of the baby behaviors that adults could learn the most from. Another: pushing food away when we're no longer hungry. Just as Will had done with his eggs that fateful morning. Babies listen to their own bodies and understand when they are full. And then, they stop.

This is another behavior I struggle with. Just the other day, my husband, Ryan, and I were eating sandwiches from our favorite place on the Upper East Side. My go-to is a total calorie bomb: an Italian hero with mayonnaise (that's in addition to the oil and vinegar it comes with). There are several kinds of meats and cheese involved. It's delicious.

And it's huge. I could easily stop after eating half. Easily. After I polished off the first half of my hero, I said to Ryan (with the other half of the sandwich sitting in front of me), "I'm having a dilemma. I'm not hungry anymore. But I really, really want to eat the rest of this sandwich. It's amazing. Or should I put it away?"

"Well," he said, "if you put it away, you know you'll never end up eating it because the bread will get soggy. So you'll just end up throwing it out."

That was all I needed to hear. On an already-full stomach, I ate another half of an Italian hero.

Controlling portions—and knowing what our stomachs can handle—is key, said Pace. "A newborn's stomach is about the size of a cherry," she said. "It grows as they grow and by adulthood our stomachs are about the size of a softball."

That hero was definitely bigger than a softball. It was maybe two-and-a-half softballs.

And what followed was feeling not only uncomfortably full but uncomfortably guilty. It's a feeling we moms know all too well.

And so, armed with this knowledge from nutritionist Pace and a righteous fire in my belly, the Baby Diet experiment began—the week of Thanksgiving no less, when diet pitfalls are everywhere. I decided I'd eat what my toddler ate, when he ate, and I'd treat my own menu with the same care I lavished on his plate each day. The food was pretty simple:

Day 1 breakfast: one scrambled egg and Greek yogurt; lunch: three chicken nuggets and peas; **snack:** grapes and crackers and hummus; **dinner:** chicken-veggie stir-fry.

Day 2 breakfast: half a bagel-thin with hummus and avocado; lunch: chicken stir-fry veggies and rice; **snack:** Greek yogurt; **dinner:** Avocado-Mexican cheese wrap.

Day 3 breakfast: oatmeal with fruit, and toast with hummus; **lunch:** couscous, and turkey and cheese mini-wrap; **snack:** cheese and crackers; **dinner:** turkey, stuffing, and green beans.

Day 4 breakfast: bacon, egg, and cheese; **snack:** yogurt; lunch/dinner: turkey, stuffing, veggies, dinner roll, cranberry relish.

The food was delicious. It was way more satisfying than the junk I'd been fueling myself with, so I actually ate less. I saved some money, because though I was feeding both of us good-quality food, it was still cheaper than the company cafeteria or greasy takeout. In total I lost more than 2 pounds in four days on the Baby Diet. I was never hungry, had more energy, and ate more well-balanced meals than I would have eaten had I not been mimicking my toddler's diet.

I was intrigued.

It was such a revelation that I wrote up the story of my experiment for my day at ABC News. I hit Publish, I patted myself on the back for half a second, and then I moved on to the next story. But my article started getting a lot of likes;

people were sharing it widely online. "What I will keep in mind about this article is that we as adults tend to forget about eating healthy and that what I plan to do moving forward is ask myself would I allow my child to eat what I am eating," said one. "It really works," said another. It was clear that this Baby Diet—and, more significantly, the concept that it was OK for moms to prioritize their own needs and desires—was really resonating with moms and others who were reading this story.

Then one of the senior producers from *Good Morning America* called me up and asked if we could turn it into a segment. I work at ABC News, but in the digital division. Once in awhile, my stories for the website get turned into TV segments. Sometimes, I'm the correspondent, but in this case, I would be the subject. But to get this kind of reaction to what I thought was a run-of-the-mill article was pretty exciting.

We shot the segment, and once the show aired, right before Christmas, I got a tremendous amount of feedback from viewers. It was mostly positive, with a few detractors who pointed out not everyone has the means to feed their children in a similar fashion, let alone themselves. I got it. But I hope the takeaway, which was my main revelation in trying this experiment, was this: that moms take so much care to give their kids the very best of everything that we don't even think about doing the same for ourselves. I don't mean that we think about it and then decide not to do it because of time or resources. *I mean we literally never even think about treating ourselves with the love and care we show our kids every day.* Or at least I didn't. And it was never clearer to me than the moment I was searching everywhere to find true nourishment—only to discover it in my refrigerator, where it had been all along.

Staying the Course

Adopting the Baby Diet for a few days, even over Thanksgiving, was actually much easier than making similar changes in the long term. I keep going back to the idea that I work really, really hard. I do everything I'm supposed to do in life and much more. Don't I deserve a little lukewarm cafeteria lasagna now and then?

I laugh when I catch myself falling into this trap, because it's so silly. The food I was eating was technically comfort food but it wasn't really a treat. It might have been momentarily delicious, but it wasn't making me feel good. And it wasn't helping me fuel my busy life, either. The days I have managed to adopt the Baby Diet since that Thanksgiving experiment proved something I already knew to be true: if I eat better, I am more productive; if I am more productive, I'm happier. Therefore, eating better leads to more happiness. Which is exactly what I'm trying to achieve.

But the trouble is, I keep failing at this diet thing. And then I feel like a failure, which makes me terribly unhappy. There are weeks and months when I'm able to adopt Will's diet for a day or two here or there, but eventually I don't plan well, end up skipping breakfast or forget my lunch on the kitchen counter, and it's back to Chipotle I go.

I decide I need to start smaller. Instead of jumping back into the Baby Diet whole hog, I'll instead eat for breakfast each day what I serve the kids. After all, if breakfast sets the tone for the whole day, then at the very least I should make better decisions if I've had a healthy start.

So I go to the grocery store on a Sunday to shop for the week. I'm ruthless: I make my decisions on what to buy based solely on what kinds of foods I will feed Will and what I would at least like for Addie to eat (keeping in mind she'll most likely eat peanut butter sandwiches). Turkey bacon; organic, free-range eggs; fresh berries; plain Greek yogurt with honey and granola become staples.

The first few days went great. Each day Will and I ate exactly the same thing for breakfast and sometimes, but not always, ate the same thing for lunch and dinner. At minimum, Addie was starting the day healthy. And again, the results were immediate and gratifying: a two-pound weight loss in the first five days. *This thing might actually work!*

Yet, try as I might, there were still those mornings I didn't have time to pack myself a lunch. But I tried not to fall into a shame spiral when that happened. I knew from my conversations with Nicolette Pace that the key to weight loss was not necessarily eating less, but eating differently. Whereas I once might wait until I was starving to think about lunch, I planned ahead and knew, by and large, what I was eating that day long before I got hungry enough to let my stomach do the Seamless ordering.

"Eat in intervals," Pace advised. Food, she said, stays in your stomach for two to four hours. So before the next time I got hangry (you know, *angry* hungry), I was already armed with my healthy food choices to stave it off. It makes sense—after all, I feed the kids in intervals: breakfast, snack, lunch, snack, dinner; 7 a.m., 10 a.m., 12 p.m., 3 p.m., 6 p.m.

But the very day I stopped eating what Will ate for breakfast? It all went off the rails. And in one day—ONE—I gained back the 2 pounds I had spent the last five losing.

Monday breakfast: scrambled eggs with cheese and a piece of toast; **lunch**: green juice; **dinner**: cod with couscous and roasted vegetables.

Tuesday breakfast: broccoli and cheddar quiche and raspberries; **lunch**: grilled chicken and spinach salad with Greek salad dressing and shredded cheese; **dinner**: three varieties of soft tacos (out to dinner with a friend).

Wednesday breakfast: broccoli and cheddar quiche and raspberries; **lunch**: Caprese salad; **dinner**: cod, couscous, and an avocado.

Thursday breakfast: Nutri-Grain bar and yogurt; **lunch**: salmon, couscous, and roasted vegetable; **dinner**: chicken salad and avocado wrap.

Friday breakfast: scrambled eggs; **lunch**: turkey/cheese roll-up; **dinner**: filet mignon.

Five days in and two pounds down. It's plain to see, looking back on the week, that I definitely didn't deprive myself. And I felt great: more energy and none of that uncomfortable-after-eating feeling and resulting tiredness. But the next day, without the structure of the weekdays, things went awry, and it all started when Will had a bowl of oatmeal for breakfast and I didn't.

One day of bad decisions had resulted in negating nearly everything I had worked for the last week. And I also felt horrible. But honestly, Saturday's food was delicious.

I got back on my modified version of the Baby Diet the next day—starting off with a breakfast that mimicked Will's and Addie's.

It was extremely annoying to me that I couldn't even deviate from healthy-ish eating for one day without paying the price. But I looked back at the week's menu and am, for the most part, proud of the food choices I made for myself and for my family that week. I had more energy and actually felt cleaner inside and out, if that's possible. It occurred to me that my road to the true Baby Diet was probably going to be a very long one, filled with detours and burrito-fueled stops as I tried to undo years of unhealthy habits.

There's more to the desire to lose weight than just feeling better and being healthier. A major part of it is vanity. Yes, I want to be thin. I'm sure you've heard that the camera adds 10 pounds, and as someone who appears on TV sometimes, I'm here to tell you that it's no joke. If you think your favorite news anchor looks slim on TV, you should see her in real life. And don't fool yourself into thinking that a woman that successful—and thin—couldn't possibly have children because far more are moms than not.

But for the person who is not being seen—and critiqued by millions each morning—weight loss is naturally less of a priority than for someone who is. A study published in 2014 in the journal *Obstetrics & Gynecology* showed one quarter of women retained more than 20 extra pounds after pregnancy—these are women who were of an average weight prior to getting pregnant. The issue is particularly common among lower-income women, who have fewer resources for child care in order to exercise and less access to more expensive, healthier food options.

So what was my excuse? I didn't have one. It occurred to me that even without one plausible reason why I can't lose the weight, I still fail time and time again. Imagine how hard it must be for women who actually have real obstacles to overcome.

But isn't the truth of the matter that we *all* have obstacles in our lives? One person might have less money but have a loving husband. One woman may have plenty of money but a sick parent to care for. One might be gorgeous but have a cheating husband. Another might have a great job but no family support around and a nanny she's not sure she can fully trust. Maybe one seems to have it all—but is suffering from deep loneliness.

No one has it all together, no matter what it looks like on Facebook.

If Momma Ain't Happy . . .

Which leads me to this book. Look, despite my detailing of my weekly meal plans above, this isn't a weight-loss book. I'm not going to give you a menu or a diet plan to follow. You'll find your own foods and portions that work best for you. But for me, eating like my baby (the same healthy foods, the same deliberate attention to hunger and satiety) really resonated. It got me thinking about something bigger than just the food I put in my mouth. I also started mulling what it was about eating good-quality food that made me so happy. And about why I was denying myself the same happiness I instinctively offered my kids every single day.

There is something that happens when we love some-one—in this case our children—so much that the pursuit of their happiness and well-being starts to become the only happiness we know. In our pursuit of parenting perfection and search for our baby's "happiness," we are losing sight of, and the time and financial resources to pursue, our own. What are the long-term implications of always putting the children first? *What if I was spending so much time focused on my children's happiness that I actually took away from it?* And what if I didn't have any left over for myself?

Today, my diet is still a work in progress. I have good days; I have bad days. But overall, giving myself the permission—even, dare I say it, the challenge—to feed myself as well as I nourish my children has been a fundamental change in the way I approach food.

And starting with that success, I thought to myself, *I can do even more.*

Embarking on the Baby Diet morphed into something quite different: tackling a series of small changes—some individually, some that are intertwined, such as sleep and ex-ercise—to make motherhood a little less stressful and a little more enjoyable. I called it my Happiest Mommy challenge, and I started diving in with gusto.

Because as the saying goes, "The days are long but the years are short." Wasn't Addie born just yesterday? No, it was almost four years ago. And those four wonderful years went by in what seems like a blink of an eye. I find myself tearing up regularly watching my kids grow, wishing with every cell in my body I could somehow stop the clock and keep them this way forever and ever.

I know I can't. They will grow no matter what I do and how much I wish for them to not.

But here's what I can do: make these too-short years the best they can possibly be, for me as well as them, so that I won't wish them to be over. So that when the kids are older, I'll look back on this time and remember it with more fondness than remorse. So that each day of this magical time can be the best it can possibly be, and we all—every one of us in this family—can be the happiest we can be and become the best version of ourselves along the way.

This book is not written by an MD; rather, it is a record of a personal journey in which I put myself through the paces of "babying" myself in several areas of life—food, fashion, exercise, socializing, and enrichment—and taking care never to lose sight of my own needs while still attending to the needs of my family.

Does getting more exercise, more sleep, going on date nights, exploring hobbies, and seeing girlfriends lead to maternal happiness? I suspected the answer would be yes. But how does a mother make herself happier while not sacrificing the happiness of her children? After all, there are only so many hours in a day and only so much energy one person can muster.

My theory is that while the list of to-dos commonly found in parenting advice columns is helpful, it's actually not necessary. Moms instead can live by one and only one rule that will transform parenting from what feels like a never-ending series of sacrifices to an all-around happier mothering experience for them, and then, in turn, for their children, too.

Do for yourself what you instinctively do for your children every day.

Chapter 2

Ditch the Playdates

Make Time for Your Own Friends

The first "playdate" I ever had with another mom will be forever burned into my memory as one of the strangest and most uncomfortable afternoons of my life.

With my first child, Addie, playdates were not something I initially gave much thought to. It didn't occur to me to seek out "mom friends." I was too busy getting my brain around being a mother and figuring out how to get through the day with this beautiful, marvelous, and needy appendage called a newborn. And so while other moms (I later learned) were joining neighborhood new-mom support groups and chatting each other up at mom meet-up groups, I mostly went about my business, taking lots of walks with my new baby and spending my maternity leave with my young family—walking in the park, going out to eat, or visiting family.

But when my daughter was about six months old, I decided to sign her (and me) up for a music class. Even at the first one, it became clear that many of the other moms in the class were already old friends. They were all friendly, but I wasn't part of the established clique. How do you know you're not in the clique in a music class for five-month-olds? Because the moms who are in the clique all set their blankets up next to each other and hold each others' kids. And don't make eye contact with you.

So when one mother started chatting me up and sitting next to me, I was happy to have some company.

Sure, she was a little strange. It was not at all warm outside yet, but she wore short dresses with no tights. She routinely bent over in class, exposing herself to the moms, nannies, and members of the kids' band at the front of the room. If her daughter crawled away from her during class, she shouted across the room for another mom, any mom to "GEEEEETTTT HERRRR."

Oddly, it never seemed to occur to her to GEEEEETTT HERRRR herself.

Anyway, when she asked if I wanted to get together for a playdate, I should have made up an excuse. Instead I invited her over to my home, where, during what remains as one of the most uncomfortable ninety minutes of my life, she shared with me in great detail the story of her insemination, the various ways child birth had changed her nether regions, and the great array of stomach issues—including flatulency—that she was currently enduring as a side effect of a medication she was taking.

Had it not been for the music class we were both in, I could have simply never seen her again. But that wasn't possible, and I had to see her every week, in fact. And music class, which was intended to be a fun activity spent with Addie, turned into forty-five minutes each week of talking this woman off the ledge of whatever happened to be on her mind any given Monday. The most frequently recurring topic was the number of vials of semen still left from the donor who fathered her daughter. There were two. While I bopped around the room, dancing with my daughter, she kept time right next to me, telling me about her ovulation schedule and possible insemination days. Instead of watching the puppet show while we sat in a circle with our children on our laps, she asked me extremely personal questions about how Addie came to be conceived: How long did it take? How often did we have to try? Did I use fertility drugs? All the while as the Baby Beethovens—the city's premiere child music group—played the background soundtrack.

We never did have another playdate, but it was impossible to ignore her. The requests to get together became escalated in both frequency and tone. I mostly blamed my job for scheduling conflicts, which seemed to keep her at bay. But one day she saw some professional family photos I posted to Facebook. She texted me at work to get more information.

Her: Hi, I saw your Facebook photos, what's the name of the photographer?

Me: Hi, it's Catherine Desmond.

Her: How can I contact her?

Me: Her website is just her name, I think all the info is there.

Her: But what is her phone number?

Me: I'm not sure, I don't think I ever spoke to her on the phone. Her email is XXXX.

Her: How could you not have her phone number?

Me: I'm actually at work right now, so I have to go. She's pretty responsive on email.

Her: YOU ARE SO SELFISH. I ASK YOU FOR ONE THING AND YOU CAN'T EVEN GET ME HER PHONE NUMBER. WHAT KIND OF PERSON ARE YOU?

Her: ALL I WANT IS NICE PHOTOS OF ME AND MY DAUGHTER TOGETHER AND YOU DON'T WANT ME TO HAVE THEM. THAT REALLY SAYS A LOT ABOUT YOU AS A PERSON. YOU ARE SO SELFISH.

Her: AND NOW YOU ARE JUST GOING TO IGNORE ME? YOU ARE SO RUDE. WHY ARE YOU TRYING TO KEEP THIS INFORMATION FROM ME?

Five-minute pause.

Her: How much did you pay for the photos?

That day I called Baby Beethovens and switched to a less convenient day and time for Addie's music class. But that wasn't the last I'd see of music-class mom.

You'd think my first screwy mom-friend experience would keep me from other playdates, but it didn't. In fact, I've gone on a playdate every single time I've been asked since. And most of the moms I meet are great—normal, interesting, funny even. But it's a huge investment of time in people who are, by and large, virtual strangers to me. One week, I had three playdates in two days, a breakneck pace of baby speed-dating even by Manhattan standards. Yet, I still have far fewer playdates than many moms I know, mostly because of my work schedule.

This would not be an issue, except for the fact that I've seen my two closest friends (who also live nearby) exactly one time each in the same time period. That translates to seeing my real, true friends a total of two or three times in four months, while seeing various people that I barely know sixteen times.

This disconnect between how I spend my time and the people who matter to me was brought into stark relief when I finally did manage to meet up with one of my best friends, Karen. We have been inseparable since we met at the pool when I was ten years old. She told me she liked my bathing suit—it was a one-piece tank with a comic-strip print. (What can I say, the girl has a great fashion sense.) From that moment on, we were besties. Every day of every summer, we were together. There was no Genny without Karen, and there was no Karen without Genny. I called her house so much that her sister just started hanging up on me. We slept at each other's houses almost every weekend.

Of course, then we grew up, we both got married, and we both got busy with work. Emotionally, we're as close as ever, but it's easy for time to slip by without actually seeing each other. When I finally did manage to make a date with Karen recently, we realized we hadn't seen each other in person for nearly five months (when we went out to dinner, drank margaritas, and stayed out too late). I expected more of the same this time, but we were both bringing our husbands.

Ryan and I walked into the bar we had decided to meet at in the East Village. Karen and her husband, Lou, were already sitting there, drinks in front of them. Big hugs all around, and then as I was about to order a drink, I asked them what they'd like. At the same moment the words were coming, I took a look at the drink already in front of Karen—and realized it was water.

"I'm pregnant!" she said, bursting with excitement. This was their first child, so this was Very Big News. After lots more hugs, and a few tears of excitement and joy, I asked her how far along she was.

Sixteen weeks was the answer. What!? How could she have kept this information from me for so long? My oldest friend, and she was already well into her second trimester before I heard the news?

"I know," she said. "I really wanted to tell you, but I had to do it in person. And you know, I just haven't seen you."

As the conversation went on, it became clear that people whom Karen was far less close to than me already knew her news. That stung. I'm supposed to be—no, I am—her oldest and closest friend. But she was right. She just hadn't seen me.

Mommy Needs a Playdate, Too

How did it get to this point? I asked myself. I think of myself as a person who prioritizes friends and friendships—I've had the same best friend for more than twenty-five years. (And hey, my kids have only known their oldest friends three years, max!) I don't want to have only Facebook friends and no IRL (in real life) relationships with those I care most about. But when I looked at how I was spending my time and who I was spending it with, the answer was clear.

I was prioritizing my kids' friendships over my own. My

kids—who were still in diapers, who mostly engaged in parallel play beside each other while I drank tea or coffee and chitchatted with a pleasant stranger—had a more robust social life than I did. How did things get so out of whack?

A 2000 UCLA study titled "UCLA Researchers Identify Key Biobehavioral Pattern Used by Women to Manage Stress" found that women need friends to ease the stress in their lives. It found that female friendships can also fill emotional needs that a person's partner in marriage often can't. The study's findings, written up in *Science Daily* on May 22, 2000, said the study also found "women are far more likely than men to 'befriend' in response to stress—seeking social contact when they are feeling stressed, with befriending methods ranging from talking on the phone with relatives or friends, to such simple social contacts as asking for directions when lost."

In other words, there's actual evidence that you need a girls' night out with your college friends.

I want to make it clear that I do enjoy the time I spend with the other moms when I take my children to play with theirs. The noncrazy moms that I have playdates with are perfectly nice. We meet at the park or at one of our apartments, and either chase the kids from swing to sandbox to slide or sit on the floor watching the kids play with each other's toys. We talk about preschools and speech therapists, what foods our kids are currently enjoying or refusing, catch up on any kids we know in common, and discuss summer schedules— camp or free time? Swimming outdoors or in? If the parents are from Addie's school, we'll discuss an upcoming event or next year's teachers.

I've gotten some really good information and encouragement

from these conversations. I found Will's outstanding speech therapist from one of those moms, and his physical therapist from another. Because of another, we've been in a play group that's hosted in the place that will become his "twos" program in the fall. And the mom of the girl in Addie's class whom she seems the most drawn to has a lot of potential to be an actual friend.

But there's only so far the conversations go. And when everyone—including me—seems pressed for time and has their guard up, the interactions stay very much on the surface. That said, the kids do seem to have a great time. But as the afternoon fades to early evening and my thoughts turn to the bottle of wine in my fridge, I realize that as much as I like these women, we're not really friends . . . yet. Because I'm not going to offer them the wine.

These people are not the ones who have been by my side through the happiest and most difficult times in my life. Isn't it those people I need to make the time for? Shouldn't *my* playdates take priority? I decided it was time to cut back on the kids' playdates and give it a try.

The Family Playdate: Not Always a Good Solution

With my new resolution firmly in place, I decided to set up my first "adult playdate" with my dear college friend Libby. Libby and I met at St. Lawrence University, when we pledged the same sorority. While I hung back a bit during our first pledge-class meeting, Libby took over on minute one of day one, putting herself in charge of composing the lyrics to our pledge song (to the tune of "Oh, What a Night").

Our friendship started slowly but intensified junior year, when we stayed on campus while many of our friends studied abroad for the semester. Libby and I just clicked, the way you find truly happens with so few people in life. By the time we found ourselves in New York City after graduation, twenty-two years old and having the time of our lives, we were inseparable.

I was the maid of honor in her wedding, and she in mine one year later. More than a decade later, the bond remains. She once took a Facebook quiz that was popular for a few days called "Who Is Your True Soul Mate?" based on Facebook activity. She got me.

But, of course, life happens. I realized that Libby had moved to a new house in New Jersey last year, and I still hadn't been there for a visit nearly twelve months later. Unacceptable. Now that I had vowed to reprioritize my own friendships, a get-together with Libby was in order.

Libby is, far and away, my most fun friend. She's my "one more drink" friend, the one that you could—and do—stay up with until all hours talking to and confiding in. But of course, now we have families and responsibilities, and getting together for a wild night isn't so easy as it was back in our sorority days. So, both of us being working moms (and the ultimate multitaskers), we decided to make it a family play-date, complete with dinner for the couples and a sleepover for the kids, at her place out in New Jersey.

The afternoon started out well. Her two girls are a little older than Addie, but they all hit it off, and Will enjoyed following the girls around their basement full of toys. The adults sipped beers responsibly and slowly while snacking on the lovely appetizers Libby had prepared.

The kids eventually sat down for dinner: Libby served homemade coconut-crusted chicken nuggets, peas, and curly pasta. It was all so civilized and respectable, a far cry from our debauched days in college. Libby's husband, John, also went to college at St. Lawrence, so almost twenty years later, there are literally no filters left among us. Nothing's off the table in terms of discussion or behavior, because by now we'd seen it all.

And so as we sat watching the kids eat, still slowly sipping our beers, I felt quite pleased with myself. Ourselves. *Look how far we've come,* I thought. *The kids definitely keep us in check. If this had been just the four of us, we'd all likely be overserved by now.*

But see, the kids go to bed around eight. And there's still a lot of time for things to fall apart post–8 p.m. Which they did. Just not in the way we might have expected.

After a few TV shows and books read by Libby, the kids were ready for bed. Will went to sleep easily, a relief since he was using a portable crib we brought along (and since, just a few weeks earlier, on vacation with my parents, brothers, sisters-in-law, and kids, he had kept the whole house awake with his screaming in protest at the indignity of having to spend the night in what he clearly deemed substandard arrangements). Addie was just so excited to sleep in a sleeping bag on the floor in one of Libby's daughter's rooms, "like a big-girl sleepover."

Kids seemingly content and presumably down for the night, we switched from beer to wine. We made dinner, sat down at the dining room table, and had a few laughs. I was really enjoying this grown-up playdate thing. That was . . . until the kids starting roaming.

First up was Addie. Turns out she was a little nervous to be at a big-girl sleepover. OK, fair enough. I went upstairs and brought her to the guest room, where Ryan and I would be sleeping later. It was the same room where Will was sleeping. I tucked her in, and she was back to sleep.

Whew. That was a close one.

Another glass of wine later, and Libby happened to go upstairs. She peeked in on Addie and saw she was dangerously close to the edge of the bed. So, being a mom herself, her natural instinct was to gently lift Addie and move her toward the middle of the bed for her own safety.

What Libby could not have known was there's a rule when it comes to Addie while she is sleeping. Never, ever, touch her or try to move her. Especially if she's in a strange bed and you are a woman who is not her mother.

I heard the screaming from their living room downstairs where I was sitting with Ryan and John. The time was close to midnight, and a quick look around the room would indicate that we should have been in bed already. Several empty wine bottles, a Cards Against Humanity game in progress, the music and the television on at the same time, and several heavy-eyed parents dangerously close to calling it a night on the sofa.

I bolted up from the couch and sprinted up the stairs. *Please, God,* I thought, *don't let her wake up Will. Don't let her wake up Will. Don't let her wake up . . .*

AHHHHHHH! WAHHHHHHH! Now they were both awake, screaming. Scared to death they would wake up Libby's kids, I got them both out of their beds to stop the screaming. Which, as every parent knows, is the surefire, quickest way to ensure that your kids will not be going back to sleep for several hours. Because now? Now it's playtime.

So there we were. Four college friends in their midthirties, all teetering on the edge of drunkenness, and charged with the task of entertaining two toddlers until they deemed it time to go back to sleep.

The next hour or so was spent alternately trying to carry on a civilized adult evening while simultaneously trying to rock a baby back to sleep in my arms while the three-year-old fought for space in my lap. There were several unsuccessful attempts to get at least one of them back to sleep, which resulted in more screaming, more trips back upstairs, more guilt about having them in a home that wasn't theirs, in a room they weren't familiar with, while I was on the verge of tears but also trying to pretend to our hosts—who, by the way, were still awake despite their own kids being fast asleep for hours—that all was well and that I had this situation under control.

It was about three when they were finally back to sleep. We had lost John and Ryan at some point in all this, but Libby, true friend she is, stuck it out with me.

I don't know about Libby, but I do know I was asleep in less than five seconds from the time I finally climbed into bed. Still in my clothes.

And then at five thirty, Will awoke, rousing not just his sister but Libby's daughters, too. The whole circus began all over again.

Later that morning, John and Libby were kind enough, despite their own exhaustion and hung-over-ness, to make breakfast for the eight of us. We sat around the table, heads in hands, barely making eye contact as we coaxed the kids to eat.

Ryan and I and the two kids left as soon as breakfast was over, because the kids have swimming lessons on Sundays. We arrived at swimming and met up with another college friend, Mike, who lives nearby and whose daughter is in Will's swim class. Ryan told me later that as soon as I was out of earshot Mike said, "What happened to Genny? She looks like she's in rough shape."

Rough shape indeed. Absolutely exhausted, my first play-date of the Happiest Mommy You Know challenge took me until midweek to completely recover from. On the upside: I spent time with Libby, John, and their kids. I got to see their lovely home. But I made a decision right there and then: from now on, my playdates would not include my kids.

Botox and Wine Don't Mix

But you know, life gets busy. I was still working full-time, still squeezing in those healthy meals I was determined to prioritize from the Baby Diet, and there are only twenty-four hours in the day. So ever the pragmatist, I decided my next friend date would involve a bit of multitasking (just not with my kids). When a work event came up on the same night I was scheduled to have dinner with my friend Chrissy, I figured, hey, why not take Chrissy with me and then head to dinner together?

And that is how I ended up getting Botox.

Chrissy and I also met in college, also in the same sorority.

In the fall of sophomore year, we both decided to join the Kappa Kappa Gamma house, but neither of us knew many people there (and I could tell Chrissy was a little uneasy, as was I). So the day of our first pledge meeting, I walked over to her dorm room, knocked, and asked her if she wanted to go together. She did.

We ended up living together for the next five semesters in the sorority house. After college, when I moved to Cape Cod for one magical summer before job hunting and joining the "real world," it was Chrissy I lived with. Our summer was filled with days at the beach and nights of waitressing followed by hitting up the local bars. I think it was that summer that really solidified our friendship, and we've been very close ever since. Chrissy and I have great heart-to-hearts, and I've spent plenty of time crying on her shoulder, and she on mine. We share a love of wine sipping and dining out, as she's always up on the latest "best" restaurant in the city.

The event was the kind of thing I get invited to frequently but hardly ever attend: beauty experts or companies hosting evening cocktail parties to get to know writers and editors, in the hopes of making a personal connection or introducing a product that could later result in media coverage.

These events, while not unpleasant, are just really not normally my thing. First, I detest small talk. Second, they are almost always after work, when I am so spent that I just want to go home. Third, they take time away from my family. Some editors love them. They've just never been my favorite.

But this particular event happened to be in midtown, very close to the restaurant that Chrissy and I had already decided to dine at. Also, it started earlier than usual: five thirty. I calculated that if we got to the event as it started, we could stay an hour and then get to dinner before seven. I could still be home by nine and asleep by nine thirty.

Chrissy does not work with me, and this was an invite-only party (for members of the media), but I told her to play it cool and go with the flow.

There was plenty of complimentary wine (which we helped ourselves to) as we walked around the spa, looking at displays for laser hair removal and fillers. We were taken into a dimly lit room to watch a woman get belly fat "frozen" off her body. Which of course required more wine.

The line for Botox was a long one. I was intrigued by how many women at this party were willing to have sharp needles stuck in their faces by someone they had had no previous interaction with.

"What are you having done, dear?" a woman wearing a white coat and holding a clipboard asked me. "Juviderm? Botox?"

"Oh, I'm not sure," I said. "Nothing, I think."

"Nothing? It's a fillers and freezers party, though," she said. "Maybe just a little Botox? In your forehead?"

And there it was. Confirmation from a professional of what I already knew. I had terrible horizontal lines in my forehead. I have been self-conscious about them for years, routinely looking at every other person who I guessed to be roughly my age's forehead to inspect what kind of lines were in *their* faces. This was a losing game. My lines were always worse.

I once had my hairdresser cut bangs to hide my forehead. But my face is kind of small, and my hair is kind of big, and so I just looked like a giant hairball. I spent hours in makeup stores looking for a kind of primer that would keep my foundation on top of my skin rather than sinking into the creases, making them look even worse.

My point is, this lady had inadvertently stumbled on a sore spot of mine.

So three glasses of wine in, I found myself signing consent forms, filling out a medical history, and being whisked into a chair while a woman who identified herself as a nurse practitioner inspected my face. Once immobilized, I saw her out of the corner of my eye, simultaneously filling up needles with a mysterious substance (that she was going to inject INTO MY FACE) and posing for photos by a professional photographer who was there to shoot the event. You know, like medical professionals do.

To say this didn't inspire confidence in me would be an understatement. But my inhibitions were just low enough (and my fear of backing out was high enough) that I just went for it. The whole procedure took about five minutes. It didn't hurt. The thing that stood out to me the most was the advice of the nurse (after I'd already been injected) that I should not lie too flat for at least five hours. Well, so much for my plan to get to bed by nine thirty for a precious night's sleep.

The thing was, during all of this craziness, I wasn't doing what I'd originally intended to do: hang out with Chrissy. Oh, she was fine—not being the type to succumb to peer pressure and also not having lines in her forehead that needed addressing, she had made some friends on the couch nearby while I was off experimenting with injectables. I realized that it was tough to concentrate on my friend while simultaneously working (even if I was only technically working). Maybe this multitasking wasn't such a hot idea. I walked over to her after I was done and promptly found out she had spilled the beans about our little ruse as soon as I was out of earshot. Oh well, it was time to leave anyway.

Oh, and as for my Botox? I have to admit, it was fabulous. The lines all but disappeared, albeit temporarily. I don't seem to have suffered any lingering side effects from having toxins injected into my face. My sleep didn't even suffer: instead of laying down in bed, I fashioned myself a comfy bed sitting upright in an armchair that night.

No Kids, No Problem

So far my attempts to multitask my own playdates with either my kids' playdates or work hadn't been a success. I got to thinking it was time to really just see my friends the same way my kids see theirs: with no other agenda or responsibilities.

With that thought in mind, Ryan and I booked flights to Kentucky. Our friends Becca and Neil had been asking us to the Derby for years. They're from Kentucky, and as such the Derby is kind of their "thing." I had secured a gorgeous hat for the event (from Libby, the night of the playdate gone awry). I purchased a new dress and shoes, got my hair blown out, and even splurged on an airbrush tan. I was going to do this up RIGHT. Two days before the Derby, we dropped the kids off at my parents' house and prepared to head out to the airport the next morning. A weekend away. No kids. No work. No distractions. No way this was going to be anything but perfect.

That is, until I went to the tailor the night before we were scheduled to leave to pick up my all-important Derby hat. I'd dropped it off earlier in the week to have them secure one of the combs, which was coming loose. But when I walked to the shop to pick up my hat, the tailor was closed. I looked at my phone: 6:57 p.m., it said. I looked at the sign of the store hours hanging in the window for all to see. Closes at 7 p.m., it said. Our flight left the next morning.

That kind of thing drives me insane. Why, if a business is not going to adhere to the hours they themselves set forth, do they bother having set hours to begin with? Ones that are posted in the window, no less? I fumed the rest of the night, but there was no way I was going to the Derby without my hat. And there was no way this wrinkle was going to ruin my perfect weekend with friends.

So the next morning, Ryan and I executed a complex plan that involved him camping out at the storefront at the crack of dawn, slipping in to pick up the hat the moment the store opened, and then barreling over to LaGuardia Airport in a cab, with minutes to spare before our morning flight. A crisis averted by a wonderful husband who understands the importance of the Derby hat.

We landed and headed for Lexington, Kentucky, where we were to meet Neil and Becca for lunch at a famous dive-style sandwich shop called Wallace Station. The ride was spectacular: miles and miles of horse farms and green as far as the eye could see. So different than the life we had just left behind in New York City.

The sandwiches didn't live up to the hype, but the company more than compensated for that. The four of us sat outside at picnic tables, sipping beer and eating, on a gloriously warm May day in western Kentucky. We caught up on life and the kids, had a few laughs discussing mutual friends, and then got back into our cars to head to a bourbon distillery on Kentucky's famous bourbon trail for a private tasting arranged by Neil and Becca—a friend of theirs is the chief bourbon taster (yes, that's a real job) at Four Roses distillery. It was everything I had hoped my weekend away with good friends could be. We gave our full attention to one another, had a lot of laughs, and really connected.

Ryan was the best man in Neil and Becca's wedding, so these are also dear, close friends we've known for so long.

The four of us spent three hours at the distillery, sipping bourbon varieties, chatting, and reminiscing. We took a tour of the distillery and learned a little about the process of making bourbon, all with no pressure and nowhere to be next. It was an afternoon that even in retrospect I couldn't imagine improving.

I imagined the next day would bring more of the same. We got up early and Becca, a true Southern belle, helped me fasten my giant hat to my head. The people who we were staying with, friends of Becca and Neil who were not attending the Derby, could not have been more gracious opening their home to us. They were headed to an amusement park that day with their children, but they left us a pitcher of the best Bloody Marys I have ever tasted in my life. The day was off to an amazing start.

Ryan and I went to the Derby with no agenda outside seeing our friends and betting on horses. But sometimes you get caught up in someone else's agenda without knowing it's happening.

When you're the senior energy advisor (Neil) to the senate majority leader (Mitch McConnell) and the event in question is being held in the home state of both that energy advisor and majority leader, there are a lot of people who want your attention. I don't think we sat down more than four times during the day-long event, and no more than ten minutes each time. We barely touched the food. We barely chatted with Neil and Becca alone for more than a moment. It was a struggle to actually watch the races, because there was always somewhere to go, someone to talk to, someone to meet. It was a fun day, a memory I'll cherish, but I was glad we had been able to spend the day prior with our friends, because there was definitely no time on Derby day to reminisce about the college days. It was like my working Botox date with Chrissy, only this time Neil was the one on the clock, and we were the ones who he was struggling to spend time with.

It occurred to me that my favorite playdates with my friends weren't necessarily the ones where we went to a fancy event or even spent a whole night or weekend together. The best ones were free from outside obligations, free from multitasking. But as we get older, the times where we're free from obligation are few and far between.

Embracing the Mom Playdate—on My Terms

With three playdates under my belt since the experiment had begun, I began to wonder what it was, specifically, that I was hoping to get out of these playdates? Does every one need to be packed with bonding to make it successful? What am I trying to come away with?

With that in mind, I made plans with Karen once more. A low-pressure, Tuesday-night, after-work dinner. We met at six and talked mostly about her baby registry and upcoming graduation from nursing school. I was home by eight, and there was nothing at all remarkable about the date.

But there's something to be said for simply making the time to see our friends and knowing they, too, made the time to see you. That, in and of itself, feels good. It's the making plans, the making time, and the spending time—whether that results in 3 a.m. child care, getting stuck with needles, or rubbing elbows with political heavyweights—that ensure the next time the shit hits the fan, those same people will be right there to help you clean it all up.

Admission: I didn't end up cutting out the kids' playdates altogether. In fact, I actually organized not one but two "moms' nights out" for the moms in Addie's preschool class. Ryan questioned my sanity, but my presence at school drop-off and events had started to feel an awful lot like that first Baby Beethoven class—like everyone was old friends except me.

Although the moms at school had been nothing but nice to me, it was clear many had become close already. There was one mom, though, and she was one on the inside—the one I mentioned earlier as the mom of the girl Addie had hit it off with—who always included me, always invited me along. She made a mental note of the days I worked from home and frequently asked me in advance if I'd like to get together on those days or join in on whatever she already had planned with the other mothers and kids. Sometimes I could join, sometimes not—but her graciousness was noted. And bonus: she was totally sane. How could I not want to be friends with her? I did.

It occurred to me that I was incredibly lucky that some of my oldest and closest friends lived within a few miles of me and that I had the means to get on a plane and visit those who didn't. Many moms are removed from their friends and family geographically and their mom friends are a lifeline at a time when many women report to be the loneliest in their lives: during new motherhood.

Millennial moms—those born between 1982 and 2004—are particularly susceptible to loneliness, despite the abundance of technology available that wasn't around for the generation of moms before them, according to the Institute of Family Studies. A synopsis of their study, titled "Millennial Motherhood: Connected but Lonely," said the following:

> "The effects of technological isolation are only exacerbated by increasing familial fragmentation in America . . . The millennial women who wind up in a new and exciting city may find they have bought flexible and interesting career opportunities at the price of raising their babies thousands of miles away from the mothers, grandmothers, sisters, and aunts who once helped form a community network of support. The same young tech-savvy mothers building start-ups through Skype meetings are interacting primarily with their own mothers, who would once be just around the corner, on Skype. And when a good nanny can cost upwards of 20 dollars an hour and daycare centers can cost $2,000 a month, even nimble millennial moms finding ways to work during naptimes can find themselves raising their children with almost no family help or support, something with little precedent in human history."

Suddenly I realize how fortunate I am. Not only does my family live nearby, but so do my friends. I realize "ditching the playdates" altogether isn't going to work for women who, like me, have no other social outlet.

I decide to open my mind to my mom friends to see what happens.

There's a mom named Sarah who lives nearby. We met in the most unusual way: I was looking for moms to comment for a story I was writing on over-the-top or unusual birthday parties. I posted my query on a popular Facebook group called UES Mommas and my in-box became flooded with responses about party planners, professional photographers, and more—typical Manhattan excess.

But one response jumped out at me. It was from Sarah, who told me that a friend of hers had thrown a birthday party for her (the friend's) daughter and had asked that people not bring gifts but instead donate to a fund to assist with medical research for a condition Sarah's son has.

I was intrigued to meet—albeit via email—another mom in my neighborhood who was parenting a child with special needs. Sarah's son is about a year older than Will, and though their needs are different, something about Sarah's heartfelt email of gratitude for her friend's act of generosity made me feel that she was someone I'd like to get to know better.

I had to meet her. But I didn't ask her if she wanted to go out for coffee. No, I asked her if she wanted to have a playdate. She did.

We met at a park. I told her how she could find me by describing my stroller.

The first date was cautious. But successful. She was lovely. And so we decided to meet again, this time at my apartment.

And so went a few months of playdates and stroller walks until one day, we decided to have dinner. Alone.

Sarah and I are now quite friendly. She has helped me in ways she will never know. Her generosity, thoughtfulness, and grace are an inspiration to me. We don't have a ton in common on the surface: we come from different religious backgrounds, she's a stay-at-home mom while I work outside the home, and we don't have one single other friend in common.

But Sarah walked into my life at the exact moment I needed her, though I didn't know it at the time. I was just embarking on a new phase of my journey with special needs parenting—I needed to increase Will's therapy sessions, I needed to start considering a two-year-old program for him—and I was floundering. Sarah guided me through it, listened to me vent my frustrations, and introduced me to the people I needed to know in order to make things happen for Will.

And in between all the heavy stuff, we bonded. We joke about the ridiculousness of the neighborhood in which we live. We chat about our husbands. We talk about anything and nothing. We check in with each other via text, and see how each other's kids are doing when some time has passed between getting together.

In other words, we became friends.

I'm not sure what I bring to the table for Sarah, but I'm very lucky to have her in my life. And had I been as rigid about my no-mom-friends mantra as I tend to be about everything else in life, I would have really missed out on a great person. And some great advice that has really benefited my baby boy.

That's what this is all about: being the best parents we can be while being the best selves we can be. For moms, you can't be one without the other.

Those two moms' night out dinners I planned? Well, as

it turns out, organizing them was one of the best things I've done in my quest to feel less like a leper at school. At the first, I happened to sit next to a mom who I had so much fun with over about four margaritas each, we became fast friends. Then Ryan met her husband, and they became fast friends. Our girls get along great, and now we see each other all the time.

At the next, I sat across from another, who said her daughter really liked Addie, and so we bonded over that, and then kept in touch, and now get together or take each other's girls frequently. Two others—one of whose building I happened to move to—also have kids Will's age and decided to join a playgroup I told them about; now I spend time with them, too, both at playgroup and outside of it.

And as for that wine in the fridge? These women are awesome. I realized that there's plenty of wine in the world, as there is love in my heart, for all sorts of friends. I opened both and never looked back.

Chapter 3

Get Sleep at Any Cost

Do Whatever Works for You
to Ensure a Healthy Night's Rest

I'm going to let you in on a secret: If you read no other chapter in the book, read this one. Because without this one, the rest are so much harder. With this issue nailed down, many of the others will fall into place without nearly as much effort.

I am obsessed with sleep. Scratch that. I'm obsessed with the sleep of every person in my household. Every single day since Addie's birth, I've had a conversation with someone, 98 percent of them being with my poor husband, about not only how my kids are sleeping but also how I am sleeping. That's almost 1,500 conversations on this topic since Addie's birth. Yes, he is a saint.

Can you imagine anything more boring than hearing about another adult's night of sleep? And yet every morning, even after all these years, Ryan asks me, "How did you sleep?"

God help him if the answer isn't a good one. Because somehow? It's his fault. I don't know how the fact that I woke up at 4 a.m. to take Addie to the bathroom and then couldn't get back to sleep is his fault. But it is.

If I slept well, though—that's good news for Ryan. Because instead of being a wild-eyed, raging bitch until it's time to leave for work, I'll be making jokes, politely discussing the details of the day ahead and what needs to be accomplished, and packing up snacks for the kids to take to the park while humming a show tune.

The obsession with the kids' and Ryan's sleep isn't because I'm so concerned for their well-being. No, it's really just pure self-interest. I'm so focused on everyone else's sleep because of its direct impact on my own. This is one area of my Happiest Mommy makeover plan where I didn't need much of a nudge to put myself or my own sleep patterns first. Nope, I've been selfishly hoarding sleep since well before either of them was born.

I Sleep-Trained My Baby and I'm Not Too Proud to Admit It

The laserlike focus on my children's sleep patterns began before I had met either of them.

I didn't know a thing about taking care of a baby, but I had heard they didn't sleep much. My brothers, each of whom has two children, seemed too exhausted to even have a conversation with me during the first several years of their kids' lives.

So I knew that in order for me to sleep, the baby needed to sleep. And being a person who treasured her sleep, I singled out sleep as my number-one baby issue.

Be damned, breast feeding. Go to hell, cosleeping. I didn't want to hear about any of it. All I wanted to know was how I was going to get this baby to sleep on a schedule. Preferably with a minimum of crying. And I'll be completely honest: if a full-fledged Ferber-esque cry-it-out technique was the only method available to accomplish this goal, I would have done it. Judge away.

But lucky for me, I stumbled upon another way. Before Addie was even born, I purchased a book called *Twelve Hours' Sleep by Twelve Weeks Old* by Suzy Giordano and Lisa Abidin. I had asked every mom I knew about their kids' sleep and was profoundly disturbed to hear that nearly every child didn't sleep through the night. Whether they were months old or years old, this seemed to be acceptable to their parents.

With one exception.

Natalie was a friend of a friend. I barely knew her, except to know that she was super type-A. Schedules, punctuality, and order were, at least from my perspective, areas she excelled in. That's the kind of gal I can get on board with. And in a chance meeting, she mentioned offhand while talking about her two kids that she used a book called *Twelve Hour's Sleep by Twelve Weeks Old* to sleep train.

My ears pricked up. If Natalie was recommending it, it had to be good.

And though twelve weeks seemed like an awfully long time to suffer with being woken in the night, some quick research suggested that if you could actually have your child sleeping for twelve hours by twelve weeks old as claimed, some sort of miracle had occurred.

I followed that book to the letter. I read, and reread, every paragraph, just to make sure I didn't miss one single step. If I missed a step, I thought, it might not work. I did everything it told me to. The book used a limited-crying solution that was reportedly more labor intensive for the parent but less gut wrenching than the cry-it-out approach.

Fine.

The method involves stretching the time between feedings so the baby eventually consumes all the food he or she needs in the daylight hours, negating the need to wake up in the night to eat. It was hard. I spent hours bouncing Addie on my knee, walking around the block in the freezing cold to distract her, singing, reading, playing until it was time to eat again.

A few times I almost gave up. But the thought of not waking every night was so appealing, I stuck with it.

Even when Ryan said it wasn't working, to just give it up because Addie was still waking up and it wasn't worth all the effort, I stuck with it. Despite my obsession with sleep, I had never been a good sleeper. This, I thought, was a gift I could give Addie that would hopefully last her whole life.

Oh, and me, too, of course.

And one night, I put her to bed at 7 p.m. and didn't hear a peep until 7 a.m. the next morning. She was twelve weeks and one day old.

I thought she was dead. I tiptoed into her room to see. I saw her back rise and fall with her breathing.

Victory was mine.

The method that I had been mocked for (it was "impossible," my mother said) had worked. I had a baby who, like clockwork, slept for twelve hours a night. Every. Single. Night.

To be sure, by the time Will came along two years later, I had a lot less time to read and reread books on sleep training. But I sort of remembered the general idea of it, and I did that. With almost no effort at all, he slept about ten hours a night.

Will is generally asleep within about one minute of being put in his crib. But now that she's three, Addie doesn't go to bed as willingly as she once did. This occurred around the time she turned three, and some sort of lightbulb went off in her head: that just because I told her to do something—like go to bed—didn't mean she couldn't push back a bit and maybe win herself another twenty minutes of hanging out with us. Darn it, these toddlers are crafty.

So I devised a routine that, for a while, seemed to calm her into a deep sleep that, unless she wakes to use the bathroom, lasts the whole night.

It started like this: After her dinner and bath, she's allowed to watch a TV show. After that, the TV goes off. We either play quietly or read a few books. Then she asks me to "make her room a spa." So on goes the scented candle to provide both dim light and pleasant aroma, and on goes the iPad on the Pandora "spa music" station to provide gentle background noise to distract her as she falls to sleep (but hidden underneath the bed so as not to distract with the light from the screen). Sounds pleasant, right?

Contrast that to how Ryan and my nighttime routine went: After the kids were in bed, we ate whatever we could find or order in (at least, until the Baby Diet piece of my plan went into action). Then I washed my face, brushed teeth, etc. We then went to bed, where our gigantic television that can be seen from space, lit up the room with episodes of *Bloodline*, while we both simultaneously watched the TV and looked at our phones or iPad.

I eventually fell asleep and Ryan then changed it from *Bloodline* to *House of Cards*. At some point I woke up and saw that he was asleep but the TV was still on. I wanted to turn it off, but I couldn't get the remote because he was lying on it and I didn't want to wake him up. So I fell back asleep, only to be woken up again at some point by the glare or noise from the TV. This time I woke him up to turn off the TV. Then, he started looking at his phone again, which kept him up for at least another hour. Eventually it's time to wake up again—hopefully before the kids—to shower, get ready for work, and prepare meals. Rinse and repeat every night.

And just a few feet away, our two children sleep in a spa room.

Why Sleep Matters

If you ask any mother to describe how she feels on any given day, the answer you will hear far more than any other is "tired." Sleep deprivation is a very real issue among parents and can color the entire parenting experience, not at all in a positive way. It's the reason for the bags under a mom's eyes that make her self-conscious about her appearance. It's why we often have a shorter fuse with our kids than we would like. It's why we can't find the energy to exercise. It's why getting dressed in anything other than black leggings in the morning feels like an overwhelming task. It's why we stay home instead of going out with friends. We are just too damn tired.

I called Lisa Meltzer, an associate professor of pediatrics at National Jewish Health and an assistant professor of family medicine at the University of Colorado School of Medicine, who is also on the editorial board of *Sleep Health: Journal of the National Sleep Foundation*. She said the detrimental effects a poor night's sleep can subsequently have on parenting are very real, and can "absolutely" have a negative impact on your children's lives.

"When parents don't get enough sleep, it affects every area of their lives, and as a result it negatively impacts their day-to-day parenting," she says. "Take a parent who works. If they don't get enough sleep, they don't perform as well at work, which in turn causes stress. They bring that stress home and can take it out on their kids. It's 'kick the dog' syndrome—taking out our stresses on innocent people around us."

In other words: Your children need not only a good night's sleep to be happy: your children need *you* to have a good night's sleep, so *they* can be happy.

This hits home. There have been days when I've sat at my desk so totally exhausted that I'm barely able to accomplish the bare minimum. One day I was so tired I left my desk, walked across the street to Central Park, and lay down in the grass in my dress and went to sleep.

Funny though—it was on those days I was actually grateful I had a job to go to rather than staying home all day with the kids. Because even when I'm at my very best, even when I've had plenty of sleep and all is right in my little world, patience is not a virtue I possess.

Take away the sleep and it gets pretty ugly.

At around the time Addie turned three-and-a-half, she

started asking for a "big-girl" bed. I initially resisted, seeing as the crib had worked so well for us all this time. But then she started climbing out in the morning and coming into our room anyway, so I figured what's the difference, and I ordered a bed.

Turns out there's a major difference. At least for our kid. Because the day that bed arrived in our apartment marked the end of Addie's three-and-a-half year run as the best kid sleeper I had ever known.

The party, as my mother says, was over.

Sure, we had had days—even stretches of days—when sleep hadn't been perfect. Or even very, very bad. They mostly centered around vacations, when Ryan and I were sharing a bedroom with the kids. Or a specific episode—like teething—that meant a lot of middle-of-the-night comforting that kept one or both of us awake.

This was different. The big-girl bed caused a full-fledged, 180-degree, sleep-regression nightmare.

After the bed arrived, she simply refused to sleep in it. The screaming was like a tribe of goats. And since she shares a room with her little brother, that wasn't going to work. I'm sure you can guess where we moved her.

Yep. Into our bed.

And so began a several-month routine of no routine at all, which, as other type-As out there will know, is almost as bad as the missed sleep itself. Not knowing what to expect each night—would I lay with her for twenty minutes? Two hours?—provoked a nightly ritual of anxiety and frustration.

It was in the midst of this madness that a fellow mom at work came to me to ask if I had any advice for her. Mary was dealing with her own daughter's sudden refusal to sleep, and my coworker, who woke around 4:30 a.m. in order to be in the city and start her shift at 7 a.m., was at the end of her rope.

"I don't know what to do," she said. "She [her daughter] just won't sleep. I was so tired last night I laid down on top of her so she couldn't get out of the bed. She was screaming and kicking, and I just held her there, I don't know what else to do."

I shared with her my own struggles as of late and recounted a scenario that had played out over the weekend. Ryan was away, so I was on my own with the kids. We had a typical day of parks and playdates. It was one of those nights that I literally couldn't fathom making them dinner—even though I was by now firmly following the Baby Diet precepts, this was one weekend I had simply forgotten to go food shopping. Call it a Cheat Day. I decided we would go out.

I gave them baths, put them in their pajamas (and then in the double stroller), and we headed down the block to Shake Shack for a tasty burger and fries. Yes, I brought them out to dinner in their pajamas. But at that point I was in no mood to change into "going out" clothes only to come home to change into "bed clothes." Who cared if it was five thirty? Not me.

So off we went. Dinner was pleasant enough. And then because it was a beautiful night, I decided to take a detour home, turning the ten-minute walk into a twenty-minute one.

It was 6:45 when I approached our building. The doorman held his finger to his lips, alerting me that the kids had, unbeknownst to me, fallen asleep. Both of them. At 6:45.

I pushed the stroller into the apartment and moved Will into his crib. Not a peep. I waited about ten more minutes and moved Addie to her—own—bed. Nothing.

I walked into my room and sat on my bed. The time? Seven o'clock. Both kids asleep. I texted Ryan my victory tale. "They're ASLEEP! BOTH of THEM!" After months of struggling to get Addie to sleep, here it was.

I may have danced a happy jig, right there in my bedroom.

"But what am I going to do," I asked my coworker the next day at work as I wrapped up my story about my glorious night's sleep, "put them in pajamas and take them on a walk every night? Ha."

She looked at me dead in the eye, not even a hint of a smile on her face, and said, "Yes. That is exactly what you're going to do."

And that's when it occurred to me. If I knew, without a doubt, that this tactic would work, I would absolutely do it. Every night.

Sleep at any cost, right?

Trouble is, I knew it couldn't work. There are obligations that keep me from getting home at the same time every night. There will be rain, and snow, and extreme heat that prevent me from this nightly walk. (Plus, neither my kids nor my waistline could stomach burgers and fries for dinner each evening.) I needed a bedtime "hack," but the Shake Shack stroll wasn't it.

There's a reason why mothers are so tired. It's lack of sleep, of course, but there's even more to it. There's a physical exhaustion that naturally comes with parenting small kids—the constant picking up and putting down; for city moms, the never-ending walking and stroller pushing; for suburban moms, the in and out of the car; for all of us the endless cleaning up; the never-ending demands for food and drink and playtime and TV shows and everything else under the sun.

Physical exhaustion is real and it is constant. But there's another kind of exhaustion that is equally, and maybe more so, intense.

In "The Real Reason Mothers Are So Tired," an article on the parenting website *Babble*, writer Chaunie Brusie writes,

> But when I stopped to think about the real reason that so many mothers are exhausted to the very marrow of our bones, I realized that the exhaustion goes more than skin-deep. Although the work of raising little ones and later, big ones, can be very physical at times, the exhaustion, for me, is also overwhelmingly within my mind. *Mothers bear the enormous responsibility of being the center of our children's worlds* [emphasis mine]—from the big stuff of life (religion, health, existence) to the small (keeper of the socks, the butterer of toast, fetcher of waters) and when I feel the weight of that threatening to crumble my very being, what I am really feeling is the burden of self-doubt when I wonder, am I good enough?

That question—am I good enough?—is always there, if only in the vaguely unsettled feeling that never goes away (especially in the middle of the night) than in articulated words.

And it's exhausting.

But it's even more exhausting, and overwhelming, and worrisome, when you're not getting enough sleep. Meltzer, the sleep expert, said a good night's sleep is at the heart of not only good parenting but peace in the home.

"Think about it," she told me. "When you haven't slept, you're a lot more likely to be snippy with your spouse." (Guilty.) "And then the bickering starts. I think we can all agree that it's not healthy for kids to see their parents constantly arguing."

All that bickering, which is bad enough on its own, leads to resentment. Which leads to tension in the home. Which leads to anxiety for parents and kids alike.

To be sure, there are plenty of other factors besides sleep that contribute to marital stress. But could many of the day-to-day annoyances and stresses be alleviated if Mom and Dad were a little more well rested?

I thought back to the days and weeks when Addie was first born: the stress of a newborn, the lack of sleep, the perception that I was doing all the work. I remember clearly one night, as I stumbled past Ryan in the hallway when I was on my way to her room to carry out the sleep training as he went to bed to rest, that I thought I might like to kill him.

I laugh when I think about it now of course. We were both exhausted. But that doesn't change the fact that, on that October night back in 2011, I wanted to put my hands around his neck and strangle him for the very act of going to bed. The lack of sleep had, in that split second, turned me into a homicidal maniac.

That was one extremely dramatic moment, but Meltzer's advice got me thinking of the plenty of times since then that lack of sleep has ruined a morning in our home.

Within a few days of my conversation with Meltzer, Ryan asked me, "How did you sleep?"

I turned to him slowly and glared. "Terribly. And if you

ask me one more question this morning, or give me one thing to do today on top of going to work, I am going to go off the ledge."

We didn't speak for the rest of the morning. But we didn't bicker, either. I'll call it a draw.

I realized I needed to, as Meltzer advised, make my sleep a priority. It was obvious that with a lack of sleep, I was operating nowhere near my best self. Not at work, not at home, not with the kids—not anywhere. I recounted to her something that had just happened on our annual Shaw family vacation to Hilton Head Island.

Addie and Will's cousins were there, of course, and so there was, as there always is when we're all together, an extreme excitement in the air. Evenings on the beach, late dinners, movies, and cousin slumber parties meant Addie was up until midnight or later several nights in a row.

But that didn't change the fact that Will still woke up at six or six thirty each morning. After all, he was in bed by seven each night. And since we were all sleeping in the same room of the house, he would wake up Ryan, Addie, and me.

So in an effort to have the kids not wake the rest of the house, I would take them out on an early-morning bike ride. But after five nights in a row of going to sleep at one and waking up at six, I was at the end of my rope.

I was riding the bike through the resort, the kids in the trailer attached, with tears streaming down my face. I couldn't believe it was 7 a.m. I couldn't believe I had an entire day of parenting ahead. The thought of taking them to the beach, the pool, out to lunch . . . was so overwhelming, I thought I might collapse right there and then.

So here I was—in beautiful South Carolina, a place I loved and had been coming to for a quarter-century, with its gorgeous beaches and scenery and my whole family there—and in that moment I would have given anything to be back in the city, at my desk at ABC News, free of the next twelve to fifteen hours of parental responsibility.

I called Ryan, who had departed halfway into our two-week vacation to get back to work, and yelled. I was angry at him, angry at my family, angry at the kids.

I was on the verge of a breakdown.

I made it through that day, and I guess Addie had finally reached her breaking point, too. We were all asleep by eight that night, and didn't wake until eleven hours later.

And that next day, everything was fine once again.

I told Meltzer about our difficulty getting Addie to bed each night since the arrival of her bed many months ago. She suggested the "Take a Break" method that involves putting your child in bed and sitting with them for a few minutes before leaving the room to accomplish some short task: use the bathroom, brush your teeth, etc. The breaks last no more than two minutes at first and then get subsequently longer.

Eventually, Meltzer said, the child learns to fall asleep on his or her own, reducing the stress around bedtime for everyone.

My Bedtime Makeover

But in the meantime, she said, I still had to figure out a way to sleep as much as possible. And so I got Ryan on board and we decided that while we were working out Addie's going-to-sleep issues, we would also work on our own.

Because as it turns out, we had just as many problems as she did.

"Did you know that the light from your iPad can affect you for ninety minutes even after you've turned it off?" Meltzer asked me. I did not.

It's true. A 2014 study from Brigham and Women's Hospital in Boston by Anne-Marie Chang, Daniel Aeschbach, Jeanne F. Duffy, and Charles A. Czeisle titled "Evening Use of Light-emitting eReaders Negatively Affects Sleep, Circadian Timing, and Next-morning Alertness" showed the detrimental effect of iPads and smartphones on a good night's sleep. It found using iPads leads to decreased levels of melatonin, the hormone that increases sleep. One dozen adults in the study were split into two groups: one that read on an iPad for four hours each night before bed and one that read printed books with a dim light. Each did this for five nights, and then the groups switched.

Not only did the iPad group have reduced melatonin, but they took longer to fall asleep, and spent less time in restorative REM, or rapid-eye movement, sleep. The iPad readers were sleepier and less alert the following morning, even after eight hours of sleep. They also displayed delayed circadian rhythms.

It strikes me that most of the iPhone and iPad reading I'm doing at night isn't because I'm reading the latest *NY Times* best seller. It's not even that I'm catching up on news I missed during the day, which I could at least pretend would somehow make me more productive at work. The truth is, when I shut down the computer and walk out of ABC News for the evening, my mind turns totally and completely to my kids. What they'll eat for dinner. Do they really need baths tonight? Do they have clean pajamas? What were their naps or lack of naps like today and as a result, what time will they go to bed?

And Mommy mode doesn't stop once they've actually gone to bed. The iPhone reading? Most of the time it's scouring for answers to questions I have about parenting—eating, sleeping, schools, development questions, playdate arrangements, school calendars, and more.

So I'm (mostly) using the iPhone because I'm trying to be a better mother. But the iPhone, as it turns out, is hampering my sleep, which, in my case, undoubtedly makes me a worse mother.

The study's findings certainly get me thinking about putting the phone away long before my bedtime. It occurs to me that I must have instinctively known all along that screens disrupt sleep—because I would never, ever, let Addie or Will take an iPad to bed.

The very thought of it is cringe worthy. Imagine, a parent who lets their child take their iPad to bed!

So why is it OK for me to do, but not OK for them to do? Meltzer asked me this very question and I had no answer. She said it was just a matter of time until they themselves would ask me this very question and demand to take their own devices to bed, too. Addie had already asked me why she couldn't have a TV in her room when her father and I did.

My answer was that when she grows up, has a job, and pays the bills, she could do whatever she wants. The truth of the matter was that her father was unable to fall asleep without the TV on, and after more than a decade of marriage, I had become the same way.

So Addie can't fall asleep without one of us in bed with her, and we can't fall asleep without the TV on. Was there really that much of a difference? We had each become dependent on someone or something else and were scared to be alone.

At least Will was still unaffected by this sleep-deprived mess we'd found ourselves in. But for how long? And I knew there was no way I could handle two kids melting down every night. I was barely making it through with one.

Like we were practicing the "Take a Break" method with Addie, I knew we, too, needed to take a break. One thing at a time.

The first thing that had to change: no more devices in the bedroom.

I knew this would be harder for Ryan than me. He is completely addicted to his phone: news, sports scores, etc.

I often wake in the middle of the night—like 2 a.m.—to find him reading nypost.com. But I convinced him to try a screen hiatus. "Honestly, what would you really even miss out on that you can't read about when you wake up the next day?" I asked. He agreed. And so each night, on our way into the bedroom, the phones get left in the kitchen on their chargers.

Ryan immediately—after just two nights—reported he was not only sleeping better but had in fact not missed out on one important sporting event or news development by allowing me to confiscate his iPhone. From my perspective, he woke up happier and was more helpful in the morning.

He also showered, shaved, and got dressed more quickly, something I hadn't anticipated at all.

Turns out that, according to Meltzer, lack of sleep delays reaction and response time. So lack of sleep makes it harder to get out of bed, then makes it harder to get in the shower, then prolongs the process of getting ready (as the person who is sleep deprived is still really trying to wake up). The other spouse then has no choice but to take on all the morning tasks—getting kids up, dressed, and fed, plus getting herself ready—in addition to anything that didn't get done the night before, like dishes.

Guess what that leads to? Resentment. Marital tension. Bickering.

Which all could have very likely been avoided by confiscating iPhones—from the adults—before bed.

And me? Getting the phone out of the room totally negated the temptation to check my email if I woke in the night, a practice that often yielded nothing but from time to time had set off my hours-long inability to get back to sleep, depending on what the in-box held for me.

Next up for Addie and her parents: a consistent bedtime.

Since the debacle of the big-girl bed's arrival, Addie had been staying up later and later. Reason being that once I went to her bed to lie down with her, there was a pretty good chance I'd fall asleep too, and since I, quite frankly, don't want to be in bed with no dinner an hour after I arrive home from work, I just put off putting her to bed until I had done everything I needed to do for the night.

We decided on what seemed like a reasonable bedtime for an almost four-year-old: 8 p.m. This meant her routine needed to start no later than 7:30, about a half hour after her brother went to sleep.

We then decided on what seemed like a reasonable bedtime for her parents: 10 p.m., lights out.

So even if it took her forty-five minutes to go to sleep, that still left more than an hour for us to eat, watch a show, and catch up for a few minutes.

No, it didn't immediately negate the need for one of us (usually me) to spend forty-five minutes in her bed coaxing her to sleep. We did get there eventually with the "Take a Break" method, which brought down the time spent in her room to a very manageable ten minutes on most nights. Meanwhile, Ryan and I had to also focus on getting as much sleep as possible in the time we had available, even if it meant sacrificing quality time together.

The first night of our strict lights-out policy for the grown-ups went well. We were in bed at about nine. We watched two shows. At 10 p.m. on the dot, we shut the TV off, said good night, and were both asleep in under five minutes.

When Will was up at six the next morning, it was fine. I was fine. I got out of bed, took him from his crib, and lay with him on the sofa until about seven. He fell back to sleep; I didn't. But when everyone else woke up, I wasn't angry. I had a night of TV-less, noiseless, lightless sleep. And I felt great.

At the risk of sounding like some sort of sleep-aid commercial, my entire perspective had changed literally overnight. My walk to work that morning was in fact very much like a commercial: instead of dreading the day ahead, I noticed birds chirping and appreciated the summer breeze.

I know this sounds insane. And if I hadn't been doing this

sleep thing so deliberately, I may not have noticed at all, just would have chalked it up to a "good morning" versus a "bad morning"—something I had previously thought was some sort of random luck.

The next night we tried it again. But this time, both Ryan and I had trouble getting to sleep. We stayed up and talked in the dark for about thirty minutes until we both eventually drifted off.

Yes, I was slightly more tired the following morning. But that time we had spent awake? It hadn't been wasted on iPads and reality TV shows. It had been spent talking and catching up in the dark, something we hadn't done in years.

That, too, felt great.

I wish I could say every night ended the same way, but the truth is, it doesn't. And there is some truth to what I told Addie about having the TV in our room—one of the privileges of being an adult means getting to make the decisions about what you're going to do when. If that means, as it does for Ryan during football season, staying up late to watch a game, then that's his right as an adult. If it means that, because I went out to dinner with friends and didn't get home until 10 p.m.—bedtime—and now I want to spend an hour watching TV to unwind, that's my choice to make.

But since the exercise in good sleep began, we—the grown-ups—have become so much more conscious of how our sleep affects our moods and our ability to parent the way we want: with love and patience. So now, an average of five nights out of seven, we're in bed at the self-imposed time. The iPhones stay outside the room and the TV stays off all night.

We made sleep a priority. It only took a minute of actually

thinking it through to realize that sleep was infinitely more important than TV watching, news consuming, or sports scorekeeping.

The nights have become more restful and as a result, the days more peaceful. That alone would have made the sleep experiment—now a way of life—worth it.

I mentioned in the beginning of this chapter that getting a good night's sleep is of the utmost importance when it comes to overall happiness. Because things that seem so overwhelming in life—like wearing actual clothes and putting on makeup, or going out with friends, or going on a run, or in the case of the near-nervous breakdown in Hilton Head, just going to the beach with your kids—are a piece of cake, and actually a lot of fun, when you've gotten enough sleep.

Chapter 4

Lose the Leggings

*Don't Let Your Style Take a Backseat
to Your Child's Wardrobe*

I can pinpoint the moment it happened. The moment I went from caring deeply about my own appearance to caring far more deeply about my kids'.

Prior to the birth of my daughter, Addie, I had shopped for the "perfect" coming-home outfit for her. Not knowing if she was a boy or a girl, though, made the search more difficult. Until I walked into BabyCZ on Madison Avenue.

Displayed on the long table of impossibly tiny newborn clothes that runs almost the length of the store was a cream-colored cashmere sweater with a matching pair of pants. It was so soft. So pure. So beautiful. So expensive.

I couldn't possibly justify the cost. I was taking a three-month maternity leave, a good portion of it unpaid. I left the store without the outfit.

But a few weeks later, on an October morning, my daughter Adelaide was born. The love of my life. The baby I had waited for. I told Ryan to call BabyCZ, describe and purchase the outfit over the phone, and have them deliver it (for an additional charge, the nerve) to Lenox Hill Hospital.

The scene repeated itself a little more than two years later. My son wore the same cream-colored outfit home from his birth, but when Christmas time came, I became obsessed with finding him an adorable outfit. The day of the first children's party of the season came and I still had nothing acceptable, though I had seen an adorable outfit that I rejected for being too pricey at . . . BabyCZ. So I called them and had the outfit delivered, this time to my apartment.

Today if you were to open either of my children's closets, you might be appalled at what you see. I get a knot in my stomach looking at the hardly worn, designer-label outfits, shoes worn once, and, for each of them, a multitude of coats and jackets. My mother always had me in an impeccable, dressy coat each winter, a gene I have apparently inherited and multiplied.

I'm not going to say that I don't have my fair share of outerwear. But my coats have accumulated over the years. My go-to black dressy jacket was purchased twelve years ago and has had a ripped lining for the last ten.

Judging purely from the complete disparity between kids' and parents' clothing I see at the playground, music class, out to dinner, this is a common issue among moms. Sure, there's the token fashionista mom at most every baby gym or birthday party—the same one who is pushing her eight-month-old on the swing in over-the-knee suede boots with five-inch heels and a fur-trimmed cape—but for the vast majority of us, it's black workout pants, sneakers, and a ponytail. And those are our "good" mom pants.

But the children? Oh, the children. Unless the specific situation calls for yoga pants—like say, a toddler yoga class—you'd be hard-pressed to find a kid at the playground in the equivalent to what mom is wearing. The overdressing of babies-toddlers-kids is definitely more prevalent among moms of girls than moms of boys, but make no mistake: a boy at a birthday party in a pair of sweatpants? Nope. Even if that party is at a gym? Correct.

Which brings me to my own darling boy. Will has, on more than one occasion and by more than one person, been referred to as "the best-dressed kid on the Upper East Side." A mother of one of Addie's friends told me that if she could take Will's wardrobe and grow the size of the clothing to fit her husband, that's exactly what she would do. I've had people I know peripherally approach me to see if they could look into his stroller to "see what he's wearing today."

Don't get me wrong. The kid looks good. But let's not pretend he has any sort of fashion sense whatsoever. He looks that way because I take the time to shop for, select, choose, and outfit him a certain way, day after day. It was the same exact thing with Addie before she began wearing a uniform to school.

And don't think that I wait until the mornings to start selecting clothing for the kids. Oh no. Each of their outfits—for Addie, her uniform most days, which is easy—is carefully selected the night before and laid out, complete with coordinating socks and shoes. The kids share a room, and each has a tiny plush chair with his or her name embroidered on it. The clothes are selected prior to the first one going to bed and then laid on their respective chairs. This is so that if, for whatever reason, Ryan gets to them before I do in the morning, there is zero chance of an unacceptable outfit being chosen, resulting in a clothing change and wasted time.

Will takes a weekly music class, to which he typically wears a button-down shirt that peeks out from under a sweater, some sort of neatly pressed pants, and a pair of socks that coordinate with the rest of his outfit. His music teachers regularly comment on his gorgeous clothes. But it's the socks that get me. Not his. Mine. Because for the entirety of the first semester of his music class—where the adults are required to remove their shoes—I did not once have a pair of socks that matched.

Every week I had mismatched socks. Every week I was mortified to remove my shoes. Every week, once class was over, I forgot completely about the fact that I did not own a pair of socks that matched, until it came time to get dressed for the next music class—even though I wore mismatched socks every other day of the week. "Buying a pair of socks that match" became something on this never-ending to-do list that existed somewhere in my head but was never accomplished, despite the fact that I was in a department store at least once every other week shopping for the kids.

I finally got some socks for Christmas. I couldn't wait for the next music class to take off my shoes. That was what it had come to for me: having my very own pair of matching socks got me excited.

I didn't used to be like this. While some women are naturally inclined to care more about clothes than others, I was no slave to fashion. In fact, I don't even like shopping. But I did make an effort to get dressed in real clothes each day and make sure nothing I was wearing had stains on it. I was also generally aware of what I had worn when and made an effort not to repeat those outfits too closely together. After all, I had plenty to choose from, so why not mix it up? But now? I was reaching a new low. I had officially embraced the Mom Wardrobe.

"I'm Not a Woman Anymore, I'm a Mom"

The idea of a "mom wardrobe" is hardly a new phenomenon. It ranks somewhere up there with the "mom haircut" on the list of things married women without children swear will never happen to them.

Professor Karen Pine, a pioneer in the area of fashion psychology, wrote a book in 2014 called *Mind What You Wear: The Psychology of Fashion* on the relationship between fashion and confidence. In it, she writes "your choice of attire has powerful feedback effects; it sends internal messages which can boost or dampen your mood and even alter your thought processes and capabilities.

"What we wear affects how we feel so much that it can distort and determine our thoughts and judgments," she continued. Pine points out that when a person is depressed, one of the first things she loses interest in is her clothing. So Pine poses the question whether or not clothing can actually serve as a mood booster. In a survey she conducted of one hundred women, nine out of ten believed the clothing they wore affected their mood.

A woman not feeling her best, Pine writes, grabs old jeans and a baggy sweater to "hide behind." She views her body as a negative manifestation of her low mood. She catches a glimpse of herself in the mirror—try as she might to avoid it—and seeing how "dowdy" she looks brings her mood down even more. So she again chooses the unflattering clothes, the mood stays low, and round and round we go.

It's not at all imagined, either. The external world picks up on the cues we send through the clothing we choose and treats us accordingly, Pine argues. In a study done at the University of Hertfordshire, forty-five people had their photographs taken and were asked questions about their mood. No one was told what to wear to the lab. The researchers, including Pine, used a tool called PANAS—or the Positive and Negative Affect Scale—a twenty-item scale to describe mood. Participants used a 5-point scale to indicate how closely words like *ashamed* or *excited* matched their feelings. Then, the participants' photos were shown to another set of volunteers. The participants' faces were obscured so as to remove any hints about mood.

"Without seeing any facial expressions, and having little more than clothing to go on," Pine writes, "there was an uncanny accuracy in the observers' ability to guess the mood of the person in the photograph. They were good at recognizing when the person was experiencing negative emotions. And they were even better at spotting when the person pictured was in a positive mood; this produced a statistically significant correlation, meaning it was more than a chance result."

The women in the study were ten times more likely to put on a favorite dress when happy than when depressed. As

Pine pointed out, it begs this question: What would happen if the depressed woman were to put on her favorite dress instead of her jeans?

This is not to suggest that I, or any other mother in her version of the depression jeans, is actually depressed. I've said it before and it's worth repeating here that despite what you might see me wearing, I consider myself an overwhelmingly happy person. But if the kids are wearing clothes that make them look great, shouldn't I try to give myself at least that much consideration?

Putting on attractive clothes, Pine writes, is likely to elicit positive behavior from others, which in turn makes us, the wearer, feel good. "We may use others as our mirror, determining how we look by the reactions we get from them and behave accordingly."

If only Will was fully aware of his status as the "best-dressed kid on the Upper East Side," he'd have enough self-confidence to take him through the teenage years.

Saturday Night Live had a skit back in 2003 that was a "commercial" about "mom jeans"—high-waisted and out of style, designed truly for function instead of form. Rachel Dratch, Tina Fey, Maya Rudolph, and Amy Poehler model the jeans, "found exclusively at JC Penney." She'll want to wear them "everywhere, from a soccer game to a night on the town," the narrator is heard saying, as Rachel Dratch and her husband head out of the house—and he looks completely disgusted.

The tagline "I'm not a woman anymore, I'm a mom" is enough to make husbands and wives alike shudder at the horrendous yet seemingly inevitable style atrocity that lies ahead.

I remember seeing that skit when it first aired. I almost peed my pants laughing, so hip I considered my young self at the time. *How sad for those moms*, I thought, seeing mothers as some sort of alien figures I could never actually picture myself becoming.

I swore that would never, ever happen to me. And while high-waisted mom jeans haven't specifically happened, their contemporary counterpart certainly has: the black workout pant. And I'm a primary offender.

Remember my routine of carefully selecting my kids' outfits the evening before? Think I do something similar for myself each night? No way. After I have their clothes selected, it's on to other tasks, none of which involve thinking about my own attire for the next day. However, I do go to an office, and proper clothing is required. So when I wake up each morning, I tiptoe to the closet and gently open the door so as not to awaken Ryan. The closet light is bright, so I don't turn it on. (I'm not alone in this—one friend with a similar apartment setup told me that she recently arrived at work with navy tights and a black dress, quite by accident. "I couldn't tell the difference between black and blue tights in the dim morning twilight," she said, laughing ruefully, "and I didn't want to wake up my husband to turn on the light and check. So I ended up walking around town all day with mismatched hosiery." It's all too relatable, right?) So I fumble around in the dark looking for something acceptable—both office and weather-appropriate—that I can wear that day. The selection is already small, and in the interest of getting dressed quickly, I usually grab something from the front of the closet. Which means I end up wearing a lot of repeats to ABC News.

But at least the kids will look good that day, right? After all, they have playgroups and naps! I only work at a major news network.

There's a *Seinfeld* episode when George arrives at Jerry's wearing sweatpants—the male equivalent of black workout pants.

George is eating a bag of chips and Jerry says, "Again with the sweatpants?"

George responds: "Yeah, they're comfortable."

Jerry: "You know the message you're sending out to the world with these sweatpants? You're telling the world, 'I give up. I can't compete in normal society. I'm miserable, so I might as well be comfortable.'"

It's not so much that moms should concern themselves with the "message" they're sending out to the world. When you're barely keeping your head above water, the last thing you need to be thinking about is some stranger's perception of you.

But instead of dismissing it right off the bat, maybe it's worth a second thought. Jerry's ribbing of George combined with the research Pine has done could potentially lead to the conclusion that when we dress a certain way, we're putting out a message about ourselves, fair or not. Then people react to us based on that message. Those reactions have the potential to color our day, our mood, whether we want them to or not.

Style Yourself Like You Style Your Kids

Putting more time into our appearance—or at least the same amount of time we're putting into our children's appearance—has the potential to improve our outside interactions and make us happier people. Even more importantly, maybe we can finally stop avoiding the mirror and actually be in those family photographs we spend so much time orchestrating.

Judging from my laundry, I was not putting out such a positive message myself. Each week, we do our family's laundry, and Ryan and I go through it and put it away—he in his closet, I in mine. Except that very little of what comes back to me each week actually needs to be hung up. Because my work clothes are primarily dry cleaned (and truth be told, worn more than once before being sent out), they come in at a different time than the laundry. Typically, my folded clothes consist of underwear, black yoga pants, black workout pants, stretchy tops, and pajamas.

"Don't you have any real clothes?" Ryan always asks, laughing. He says it nicely, to be fair. And it's an ongoing joke that unless I'm going to work I'm not "getting dressed."

There are days, of course, when I do try to put my absolute best foot forward. One event stands out in particular: the day of Will's baptism. It was going to be perfect. I ordered a beautiful cream-colored dress with a blue collar and cuffs. It was selected meticulously for the white (baptism) and the blue (baby boy). The silhouette—sheath—was chosen to hide the 10 pounds I had not managed to lose since he was born five months earlier.

That morning I managed to get myself to the Dry Bar two blocks away for a blowout. I even managed to make it to the nail salon for a quick manicure and still make it back to the apartment in time to get Will dressed in the family christening gown, perfectly pressed and pristine. He was still a bit of a spitter-upper at the time, so I waited until the last possible second to dress him, and then pull on my own dress, before walking out the door. I had planned to wear my nude-colored heels, but they were nowhere to be found.

I started to sweat. Now the whole family was dressed and waiting for me to find my shoes. Aren't the kids the ones who are supposed to be losing shoes all the time? Nope—their shoes had been laid out in advance in order to avoid the exact situation we were in at this very moment, but it was me who was about to go shoeless. We had to leave. I had no shoes. After a string of expletives came out of my mouth (yes, I know we were headed to church), I regained control and put on a pair of black shoes. I realized the nude shoes were sitting under my desk at ABC, but I decided I would not let such a silly thing color the day. This was much bigger than shoes, I thought, and really, the black ones were fine! No one would be looking at the shoes anyway. Who cares!! There were almost fifty people coming to the church and following luncheon. No time to worry about shoes.

As it turns out, I shouldn't have worried about the shoes at all. What I should have worried about was the control-top pantyhose I was wearing. In every photo from that day in which I am standing and holding Will, which is most of them, since much of a baptism consists of standing and holding the baby, the control top from my stockings is showing from the bottom of my dress. In every single one.

But Will? He looked like an angel. Though I don't think he cared.

It has come to the point where I avoid opening Will's closet, because of the clothes I see that he has already grown out of . . . without ever wearing them. (That's right: I'm turning my baby into a cliché from *Clueless*.) The tags stare back at me, black prices jumping off the white background to punch me in the gut: $40 sweater. $60 pants. An $80 jacket. His closet has become a source of shame, a reminder of money completely wasted.

Mom has nothing to wear. Meanwhile the kids—who are growing and changing every day—have enough too-small clothes with price tags still attached in the closets that opening a baby boutique starts to seem like a reasonable option.

I contemplate having another child so he (if it is in fact a he) can wear the unworn clothes.

In the interest of putting the kids first, Mom often gets dressed second. Mom decides she can't worry so much about her own appearance (after all, she's a mom) and hopes that everyone else's attention, much like her own, will be focused on her offspring. Somehow Mom, in perfecting her child's appearance, feels like she failed when it came to her own. And no matter how hard she tries to not care, it colors the day. Mom feels less beautiful than she hoped and looks back on the photos and wishes she had remembered to put on mascara.

I wish I could say I learned my lesson after the baptism debacle. But I didn't. We planned to take the kids to a pumpkin farm that fall to select pumpkins for Halloween, pet animals, and take hay and pony rides. How fun, right? How many photo opportunities! I imagined the kids, knee-deep in pumpkins and the perfect fall photos that would ensue.

And so I got to thinking about their outfits. Addie had the perfect one. Ralph Lauren riding pants, complete with knee patches, a tweed Ralph Lauren blazer—yes, a blazer for a three-year-old—and a white button-down. But, I thought, there was a problem. Clearly she would need riding boots to complete the "look." So off I went, in search of riding boots.

Now onto Will. Obviously his orange cashmere sweater with the navy blue elbow patches! Why there is so much cashmere available for kids under two I'll never know, because young children are known for neither their cleanliness nor their respect for expensive items. Still, it's almost impossible to resist putting such a soft little baby inside a piece of such soft clothing.

I guess that's why. No one can resist. At least not me. He also has several pairs of cashmere pants. Not exactly practical. But again, hard to resist.

So there they were, dressed to the nines. Addie even let me put a large bow in her hair.

And then there was me.

It never occurred to me that I might like to be in a photo with them, too. Or that if I was in a photo, I might want to look presentable. I think I am in one photo from that day, and though that felt like one too many at the time, I'm glad it exists. Because it serves as a reminder of how completely out of balance things were at that moment.

I couldn't even be bothered to put on a pair of jeans. Yup, I was rocking the ubiquitous black workout pants.

If you're getting dressed to go out with your kids one day, and it feels like even too much effort to put on jeans . . . that's when you know it's time. It's time to reevaluate what's going on in your life, because chances are there's something that needs addressing.

For me, it was total and complete exhaustion. I was too tired to button a pair of pants.

Covering lifestyle topics—including some fashion, which never ceases to make me laugh out loud—I have the luxury of spending some time at work searching for answers to common "lifestyle" problems. Including my own, of course. And my problem was that I need some help with my clothes, stat.

There have been several "solutions" to this problem in recent years. One is renttherunway.com, which allows you to rent designer dresses and to a lesser degree, everyday clothes, for a small fee, and then simply return them when you're done. It really is primarily directed toward special-occasion dressing, but I thought that I could potentially use it for a better selection of work clothing, which for me often involves a dress.

My first order was a royal blue dress, sleeveless but professional. It had a fitted top and a flared skirt, a silhouette I had come to favor over a fitted-all-over style. The dress was less than impressive and in retrospect looked far better on the model than it did on me. Still, it was a new dress for me, had cost only $35 to rent for a period of time, and meant I had one less thing to think about one morning before work. That alone seemed worth it.

The trouble came when it was time to actually return the dress. The instructions that came with the dress for returns were actually crystal clear, but because of my lack of experience with UPS boxes, it turned into an hours-long event for me.

I went to the UPS website to figure out where I could find a drop-off box near my office on the Upper West Side, and I was so pleased to find out there was apparently one right across the street. Fantastic! So I brought the dress to work in the preprovided return packaging and planned to return it when I stepped out for a bite for lunch.

I walked to the corner of 67th and Columbus and looked for a UPS box on the corner. No box. That's weird, I thought. So I looked on the website and it seemed there was one just a few blocks north. OK, I thought, *I'll just walk to the next one. Maybe the website is out of date and this particular UPS box is gone for some reason.*

More than an hour (and several fruitless stops around town later, lugging a big box and getting ever-more-nervous about my seemingly endless lunch hour), I was finally clued in by a kindly stranger to the fact that UPS drop boxes are often located inside of buildings. Whoops.

By the time I got back to work—located, by the way, directly across the street from an office building that had a UPS drop box inside, just as the website had indicated—two hours had passed. And though none of this was the fault of Rent the Runway, I decided I actually hated Rent the Runway. Forever.

So that was that.

Still, I was determined to dress better. *Good Morning America* did a piece on a company called Stitch Fix, which is essentially a subscription-based service for clothing. It sounded pretty simple—fill out an online questionnaire, and clothes that match your style will arrive at your door. Keep what you want, return what you don't. Like a personal shopper for people who hate to shop. Perfect, I thought.

According to the company, 70 percent of women who get their first box of clothes get another within ninety days. And I know personally many women who are Stitch Fix subscribers and love—love—it. I was not one of those women.

It took some time to fill out the profile. I thought I communicated my needs well—a mix of professional and "play" clothes favoring a classic, tailored look. Nothing boho, nothing too trendy, nothing too preppy.

To be sure, there was nothing "wrong" with the clothes that showed up at my door. I actually kept the jeans that came; they were supersoft. But the navy-and-white horizontal striped T-shirt, the loose-knit sweater, the red dress with the faux-leather black detailing—not for me. So back to the company it went.

For someone who doesn't give a lick about fashion, it seems that when I decide to take off my yoga pants I'm pretty particular.

The truth was I liked many of the things I already owned. But they were hidden among the clutter of dresses that were too young, skirts that were too short, sweaters that were too pilled. It was time to clean out the closet.

Seven bags of donated clothes to Goodwill later and at least I knew what I had. Turned out I had plenty to wear to work but not much in the way of weekend wear, save for that pair of jeans I had kept from my ill-fated Stitch Fix experiment.

So with the mantra of treating myself the way I treat my kids in mind, I headed back to the place where the unraveling of my wardrobe and the start of theirs began. Madison Avenue.

But exorbitantly priced cashmere jumpsuits were not on the shopping list. Madison Avenue, famed for its designer boutiques, of course, is also home to much more accessible brands like J. Crew and Ann Taylor. So that's where I began. A slave to fashion I'm not—at least when it comes to my own clothes—so it was with basics I began. Still, actual pants with buttons and blouses instead of T-shirts was a major step in the right direction.

While selecting my new wardrobe staples, I thought to myself that I'd likely have to spend more time taking care of these clothes than I did my current mom wardrobe. I wouldn't likely ever wear the silk shirt I was holding to bed, for example.

A lightbulb went off. I sometimes wore the clothes I had been wearing all day to bed. Now, to be fair, I always changed into a clean pair of workout pants when I woke the following day. I'm not a total barbarian. But if the clothes you wear during the day can also double as pajamas? Yeah, that's not OK. Remember the "pajama jeans" commercial? "Pajamas you live in," is the tagline. I was repulsed by the pajama jean. *What kind of society are we living in*, I thought, rather smugly, *that people can't even be bothered to get dressed anymore?*

Apparently that society that so repulsed me was actually, well, me. No, I never ordered a pair of pajama jeans, but how far off was wearing your workout clothes to bed?

Prioritize Your Own Closet

So once I realized that I had clothes to wear to work (and once I could see them again, after I'd lugged the many bags of discarded clothing to Goodwill), I realized that, as in all other aspects of my life, I had to treat myself as carefully as I treated my kids. Luckily, the solution here was simple: I decided to simply start laying out my clothes the night before, exactly the way I do for the kids. After all, selecting my clothes in advance takes nothing away from them, right? I would spend the three minutes I would have spent refilling a water bottle or filling yet another cup with goldfish instead selecting my clothes for the following day.

It's often the simplest things that make a huge difference. I try not to be a superficial person, but it would be nice to look nice when I go out in the world each day. And the simple act of choosing my clothes—complete with socks and shoes—in advance allowed me to do just that.

It also helped me in the mornings. No longer was I rustling around in the dark, grabbing mismatched shoes, and silently cursing at Ryan for still sleeping. I simply got out of bed, grabbed my clothes I had laid out nearby, and headed to the bathroom for thirty uninterrupted minutes of showering and getting dressed. I emerged from the bathroom fully ready for the day—makeup and all—before the kids were up. Now I was able to concentrate on making sure everything they needed to do was done before they headed out the door: breakfast eaten, teeth brushed, snacks and lunch packed for the day, and often even getting their dinner plated and in the refrigerator to cut down on the "What are we eating for dinner?" chaos that typically ensued as soon as I walked in the door each evening.

This act of laying out my own clothes proved so successful that I decided to figure out what else I could do each night to make the mornings easier. I was already packing Addie's lunch and snack, and decided to do the same for Will. I realized that the last few minutes before we had to leave for school drop-off and work were by far the most stressful of the morning, because shoes were not on and hats and mittens needed to be found. Now, if I could make the kids sleep in their shoes, I would. But that didn't seem fair, so instead I had them out when they got dressed, rather than having them walk around shoeless until the last possible minute. It didn't jibe with my no-shoes-in-the-apartment preference, but the stress it ended up saving us was worth it.

I also decided on what mode of transport we would be

using to get to school the night before. Now, suburban moms travel by car, always. But in the city, there are a multitude of ways we might walk to school other than just simply walking. If it's a day when just Addie is being dropped off, she could walk or take her scooter. But the scooter can't be left at school, so that also has to be a day when I have time to stop back at the apartment on my way to work to drop it off. If it's a day when Addie is being dropped off and then Will is going to playgroup, we have to take the double stroller. If it's a day when Addie is going to school and Will is going to his "twos" program, that means they are getting dropped off separately and we need to bring Will in the single stroller, because the stroller has to be left there for my mom or our sitter (depending on the day) to take him home in, and the program does not allow double strollers to be left there. Phew!

It's enough to make your head spin. But the thing is, better to have your head spin when you have the time to think through an issue, than, for example, in the morning when the clock is ticking and the stress is mounting and you can't find the rain-cover for the stroller.

The truth is, I hated who I had become in the mornings ever since Addie started preschool. Snippy, angry, and, on some mornings, downright nasty. It seemed no matter how early I got up, when it was time to leave at 8 a.m., we were still not ready. Inevitably, the mornings involved yelling and sometimes tears. An argument with Ryan. And by the time I got to my desk at work, I was emotionally and physically exhausted.

It didn't escape Addie's attention. On the morning—the very first morning—I had implemented all my new tricks, things went off without a hitch. In fact, I was able to sit on the couch with Will and watch *Yo Gabba Gabba* for ten minutes. I was able to joke around with Addie and take a leisurely walk with her to school instead of dragging her down the street.

And she said to me—in all her four-year-old wisdom—"I'm glad you're not mad at me today, Mommy. I love when you walk me to school."

It was heartbreaking. But it was a wake-up call. She deserved better. Will deserved better. Ryan deserved better.

I deserved better.

And better is exactly what I got. That day, when I arrived at work, I was cheerful. Instead of reliving all my shortcomings of the day so far, I quickly settled into my desk, made a few jokes to my coworkers, and felt . . . happy.

Laying out my clothes the night before wasn't the total answer to morning bliss. But it certainly helped. And in keeping with my motto of simply treating myself with the same care and consideration as I treated my kids, it fit right in. Their clothes laid out, then mine. Everyone wins.

Chapter 5

Love the One You're With

Treat Your Husband as Kindly as You Treat Your Kids (and Your Barista)

Tears, viselike hugs, and promises of a quick return.

My reaction to being away from my husband for any extended period of time was, at one time, not unlike the reaction my three-year-old has when I leave for work after being home for a few days with her.

In other words, there was a time that leaving my husband made me actually sob like a baby. About a year after we were married, I was invited on a last-minute trip to Kuala Lumpur. I was just beginning my travel writing career, and there was no way to say no, nor was there any way to bring him along.

We hadn't left each other's side for more than a night since we had been married. We were largely attached at the hip, preferring even when we were out with our many mutual friends to spend time together. The thought of leaving him for several days, and being so far away, ripped open my heart.

He drove me to the airport and every mile closer I filled with dread. I was about to board a first-class flight to an exotic place I'd never been and yet the only thing I wanted was to head back to our tiny apartment in Murray Hill and snuggle up on the couch with Chinese takeout.

At the airport, as we said good-bye, I sobbed. Like, heaving sobs. Trouble-catching-my-breath sobs. I must have hugged and kissed him a hundred times before I finally left. While I was gone, I thought of him constantly and my heart actually ached with how much I missed him.

It occurs to me now that while I manage to keep the tears in check in front of the kids, this is pretty much exactly how I feel when I have to leave them for a night.

As I mentioned earlier, I met my husband, Ryan, while we were both in college at St. Lawrence University. Having the same group of friends meant we had known each other—and been hanging out at least weekly—since our sophomore year. But things didn't turn romantic until just a few weeks before graduation.

It was shocking to me both then and now how much I loved him and how fast. We talked, and talked and talked. We'd spend the evening at the college bars with our friends, leave around midnight, and then stay up talking until five in the morning. It only took about three weeks before "I love you"s were exchanged.

By the time we fell in love just a few weeks before we were to graduate, we both had postcollege plans in place. I was moving to Cape Cod for a few months, followed by plans to travel in Europe in the fall; he was going to the Bahamas and then on a cross-country road trip and had a job waiting for him in Boston come September.

The thought of being away from him was too much to

bear. I made up a story about going to the Bahamas to visit my friend Chrissy from college and begged my parents for money for the plane ticket. (Even though I was twenty-one years old at this point, there was no way I could tell my parents I was flying to the Caribbean to stay with a man they had never met. Not on their dime.) When I got off the plane, Ryan met me at the airport with a Bahama Mama in hand, and we spent the next few days falling even more in love.

Life took us to separate cities after that summer—he to Boston for the job, me to New York after the Europe trip for a job at NBC. After a year of traveling up and down I-95, it was time for one of us to move. That person was me. A few years in Boston followed and after a failed stint at a mutual fund company, I decided to get a graduate degree in journalism because really, it was time to get my act together and it seemed like a respectable enough profession. Most importantly, it was not a job at a mutual fund company, which was eating away at my soul every time I pulled on the required skirt suit and closed-toe shoes with pantyhose. We were engaged shortly after I graduated and then it was time to go back to New York, my city, where my family lived.

Ryan and I were married for seven years before Addie was born. And if you think that spending day in and day out with the same person for seven years (not to mention an additional few years of dating and engagement) would be boring, think again. It was wonderful. The thing about Ryan and me is that we truly, deeply enjoy each other's company.

Like maybe more than is normal, I've come to realize. We love our friends, of course. But we are equally as happy out to dinner, or at a bar, or at a party full of people we don't know, or sitting on the couch, or on vacation, or really any-where . . . alone.

Similar scenes to the Kuala Lumpur event repeated them-selves over the years. Tears (mine) and hugs at the door to our apartment when one of us had to go away for a night. Otherwise, I made him breakfast each morning and we would sit and chat before we left for our offices.

We jokingly referred to it as our "morning meeting," though in retrospect before the kids came along, there wasn't all that much to discuss outside of what we might feel like doing that night for dinner. We talked all day over email and raced home at night to see each other.

These days, the scene at our apartment when I leave for work in the morning is still both gut wrenching and dramatic. It's especially bad if I've been home for a few days and then have to leave. But now the tears are the kids'.

First Addie starts with the delay tactics: "Mommeeeee, I need millllkkkkkieeee!" as she sees me look for my jacket. "Mommmeeeeee, help meeeeee get dressed," she pleads, despite my having been trying to get her dressed on and off for the last forty-five minutes to no avail. And then finally, the tiny voice says, "Mommy, I don't want you to go to work." Then the tears and the clinging to me. If it wasn't my own wonderful and extremely loving mother staying with them while I go to work, I would seriously wonder what was happening with their caretaker once I left for the day.

We hug, we give many, many kisses, we give high fives and say "I love you" over and over and make promises to talk during the day and then talk of what we'll do when I come home that night.

And talk to her I do. And to Will, who my mother says tries to kiss the phone when he hears my voice. At least three times a day from the office. I sit in an open newsroom and am definitely the only person who takes and makes multiple personal calls each day. But in an age when we're always "on", the line between work and home becomes more blurry. So the calls continue.

And then I race home—to see my kids.

And when I do—the joy is enough to make my heart explode. I open the door and before it's all the way open I hear the feet come running my way. Finally it's open and Addie yells, "Mommmmmmmmeeeeee!!" as she throws herself into my legs, hugging me so hard I can't get inside. Nearly every day she's made me a picture, or picked me a flower or perfect leaf, or found an especially pretty rock. Just for me.

Will has a similar reaction. He sees me come in and tries to physically leap out of the arms of whoever is holding him to get to me. Sometimes that person is Ryan.

I hug it out with Addie and then rush over to Will. I scoop him out of Ryan's arms, hug him, kiss him at least ten times, tell him how handsome he is and how much I missed him.

Sometimes Ryan and I exchange a kiss on the cheek. Many times we don't—it actually feels a little awkward. One of us says, "How was your day," the other gives a nondescript "OK" or "Good," and we start in on the nightly routine.

If I get home before Ryan, the scene plays out much the

same way. Kids first, then me. It hurts a little, but believe me, I totally get it. But is it OK?

Ryan and I have a wonderful marriage. Especially when I hear others talk about their own. But I'm shocked when I talk with people who seem to have actual contempt for their spouses. That's not the case with us.

I worry, though, that I neglect Ryan and take him for granted. This is something that troubles me tremendously—simply because of how much I do truly love and appreciate him. I know our lives are far more chaotic and stressful than they used to be, but I am totally committed to staying close, not growing apart.

Patience Is a Virtue—and a Necessity

One morning at Starbucks, I was placing my usual order: "May I please have a grande in a venti cup vanilla ice coffee with extra room? Thank you." The barista didn't quite follow. I gently and politely repeated my order. Again, didn't quite get it. She apologized. I assured it was more than fine and repeated it for a third time. That time, she got it. I smiled, thanked her again, and walked to the counter, where I would retrieve my coffee in a few short minutes.

I despise repeating myself. This is unfortunate, because Ryan is often deep in thought, and when I tell him something and I can tell it didn't quite register, I will ask him, "What did I just say?" If he admits he has no idea, into a rage I go.

It's infuriating. The truth is that Ryan's the talker in our relationship, not me. In words spoken between us per day, he easily out-words me by three to one. So in my mind, if I deem something important enough to say out loud, I expect that he should listen.

The Starbucks scene was not out of character for me—I pride myself on having excellent manners, treating people with respect, and being courteous to strangers. But had Ryan forced me to repeat myself three times on a busy morning when I was trying to get to work, I would have lost it on him.

It occurs to me that I have been treating the Starbucks barista—who I don't know—with more courtesy than I've been treating my own husband, who I love more than anyone in the world.

I decide that, going forward, I will be as polite to my husband as I would be to the Starbucks barista. And I'll be as patient with him as I am with my children.

And it turns out gratitude may just be the key to a happy marriage. A 2015 study from the University of Georgia called "Linking Financial Distress to Marital Quality: The Intermediary Roles of Demand/Withdraw and Spousal Gratitude Expressions," authored by Allen W. Barton, Ted B. Futris, and Robert B. Nielsen, found "feeling appreciated and believing that your spouse values you directly influences how you feel about your marriage, how committed you are to it, and your belief that it will last."

In other words, two little words may hold the key to a happy marriage: "Thank you."

Gratitude, which can be a tough emotion to muster up in times of marital stress, is particularly important when things get tough in a relationship. While financial stress, for example, might cause one or both in the couple to become more critical or withdrawn, gratitude "can interrupt this cycle and help couples overcome negative communication patterns in their relationship, patterns that may be a result of current stressors they are experiencing," a press release about the study stated.

The study authors also said that it's not about how often a couple argues, but rather how they argue and how they treat each other on a daily basis. Ryan and I are true partners in every sense of the word. We've figured out over the years who is good at what, and now, without discussion, we each handle those things. In general, I'm the big-picture person and he is the executer of the details.

So when we decided to move into a new apartment (which ranks right up there as one of the most stressful life events imaginable), just as I was undertaking this Happiest Mommy experiment, I knew it was an opportunity to practice what I was preaching with Ryan. But the truth is, we are just really bad at moving. No one enjoys moving, of course, but I can't help but think we have been worse at it than most. Two people who despise messes, disorganization, and chaos are not at their best in a situation that absolutely promises to offer all three.

But it was a necessity, and so we fell into our respective roles: I, the big-picture person, found the apartment we would live in. Ryan did literally everything else. He dealt with the price negotiations, hired the movers, changed our address with the post office and on our bills, coordinated the move-out/move-in dates with our current and future buildings, handled all the finances, hired the handyman who would move my precious light fixtures from one apartment and hang them in the other. He had the cable/Internet company lined up for the morning of the move so I wouldn't miss a beat at work or any episodes of *Real Housewives*.

And in the weeks leading up to the move, knowing how much pressure I was feeling from the weight of all that was happening around us, Ryan never mentioned a word about all the work he was doing to make sure our move was seamless—which, for the first time, it was.

So that evening, on the first night in our new place, surrounded by dozens of unpacked boxes that never seemed to empty, I decided I would tell him how grateful I was for all the work he did.

"Hey," I said, "I just wanted to say thank you for all the work you did to make the move as stressless as possible. I really appreciate it. I know you were stressed out about it and it was so great of you to just handle it and not let on all that was going on to make this happen. I love you."

"You're welcome, babe. I love you, too."

And with that simple, fifteen-second conversation, the mood in the apartment changed and immediately became lighter. Instead of frustration at all the work still left to do to make the place livable for the kids (who were with my parents and due home the next day), we decided together to concentrate on getting our bedroom done so we had a place to sleep and putting away anything dangerous so no little people could hurt themselves.

We unpacked until about 10 p.m., when we finally collapsed on the couch and ordered a pizza. We watched the

TV Ryan had made sure was hung in its proper place, turned on our favorite shows via the DVR that he had made sure transferred from our old apartment, and promptly fell asleep.

A week later was my birthday. Ryan got me a card to go along with my present. This is quite unusual for him, as while he is quite thoughtful when it comes to gifts, the simple act of getting a card to go along with it isn't something he generally does.

"Oh, you got me a card this time, too?!" I said as he handed me the box. The white envelope simply said "Genny." I opened it.

> For all the times I forgot to say thank you; I love you; I don't know where I would be without you . . .

And on the inside:

> Thank you.
> I love you.
> I don't know where I would be without you.

I have a box in my closet that I keep all my greeting cards in. I don't know what I'm saving them for, to be honest. But this card from Ryan—I keep it on my dresser and look at it a few times each week. Especially if I'm feeling underappreciated.

The negative effect of marital discourse on children is well documented. In researching the various chapters of this book, it seems that a happy marriage is the most critical ingredient for raising happy kids. (I know I also touted the great importance of a good night's sleep, and I stand by that, but I feel these two things are closely related: we cannot possibly be our best selves, or the best partners, if we are exhausted. In my experience, I am the very worst version of myself when I am not sleeping, and therefore, the very worst version of myself as wife and mother.)

Though divorce is, in many situations, unavoidable, there's plenty of research to back up the idea that the children of married parents fare better than those who break up.

Unfortunately, the negative effects of marital stress start taking their toll on kids at a shockingly young age, and again, sleep comes into play. A 2011 study of more than 350 adoptive parents titled "Longitudinal Associations Between Marital Instability and Child Sleep Problems Across Infancy and Toddlerhood in Adoptive Families" showed that poor sleep patterns in children from ages nine to eighteen months are likely influenced by conflict in their parents' marriage.

The researchers chose to study adoptive families to rule out the possibility that any ties between parents' behavior and children's sleep were due to shared genes. The children whose parents experienced marital instability when the children were nine months old also had sleep problems when they were eighteen months old, regardless of temperaments, parents' anxiety levels, and birth order.

That said, adjusting to a new baby and erratic sleep patterns is not going to have a positive effect on anyone's marriage. After all, the only time I seriously considered committing homicide was in the first few weeks of Addie's life while I wandered around the apartment in circles trying to calm her to sleep while Ryan stayed in bed, asleep and blissfully unaware of the plot to kill him that was forming in my sleep-deprived brain.

Sleep is one thing, and perhaps related to a multitude of other issues that could come up, but there are far more serious effects of marital stress on children, even in very young children.

A study of fifty couples with three-month-old infants found that the babies of unhappy marriages showed a markedly lower capacity for joy, concentration, and self-soothing than babies whose parents had thriving relationships. These couples had been part of an ongoing study by Dr. John Gottman, clinical psychologist and cofounder of the Gottman Institute with his wife, Dr. Julie Schwartz Gottman, and world-renowned for his forty years of therapy and research in the areas of marriage and parenting.

He also videotaped these parents playing with their babies, and he found that the couples weren't in sync, either: they weren't smiling or including each other much in the interaction. It's not that the couples were fighting at that moment, but their babies nonetheless picked up on the tension. How does he know? The babies had an actual physiological reaction—an accelerated heart rate.

In another study, Gottman's research team took hourly urine samples of sixty-three preschoolers over a twenty-four-hour period. The three- and four-year-olds who were being raised in homes with what Gottman characterizes as "great marital hostility" had markedly higher levels of stress hormones than those children whose parents' marriages were stable.

What are the long-term health consequences of a marriage filled with strife on our children? It's hard to say until the children are grown. But the behavioral consequences are easy to see: Gottman's study followed the children through age fifteen, and the kids of the troubled marriages had a significantly higher incidence of truancy, depression, peer rejection, low school achievement, and behavior problems—especially aggression.

One of the most pervasive pieces of advice when it comes to finding marital happiness after kids is having "date nights." And while there's nothing wrong—and in fact much to be gained—with getting a sitter and going out with your significant other in the same way you might have before kids, it must be recognized that this is not a financial reality for many people. Even if you're lucky enough—like me—to have family close by who is always willing to help, the expense of the actual going-out isn't always possible.

This past summer, Ryan and I had every Tuesday night to ourselves. The kids stayed at my parents' apartment from Tuesday morning until we picked them up after work on Wednesday night. Ten Tuesdays in a row. We did do a few fun things—like going to an Italian restaurant in the neighborhood that's not at all stroller friendly and seeing a performance of *The Tempest* during Shakespeare in the Park. But more often than not, we chose to simply meet at home, order takeout, and sit on the couch enjoying the quiet and the long-lost pleasure of eating an uninterrupted meal. There was also the added benefit of being able to go to sleep and not worry about what time a certain three-year-old would come in to be escorted to the bathroom. It is utterly baffling to me why a child who is perfectly capable of using the bathroom by herself during the day completely loses this ability at night and requires an audience. But there you have it.

Our friends were, to put it mildly, jealous of our every-Tuesday break from parenting. And truth be told, I practically skipped home from work that night each week. But while our date nights were indeed blissful, I'm not sure they offer much long-term assistance in the stress that necessarily comes with parenting. Nights out with your spouse and nights off from the kids are a break from reality—a much-needed one, quite often—but they are not the reality we live in. So as soon as the night is over, it's right back to real life.

It occurred to me then, that rather than breaks from reality, it was far more important to focus on making the reality—our actual day-to-day lives—better. To make our marriage the best it could possibly be all the time.

The Importance of "Just Checking In"

It's crucial to build up the relationship during the good—or at least the calm—times so that if and when things get tough, whether it be financially, medically, or the million of other possible stressors put on a marriage, there's a solid foundation of mutual appreciation, respect, and love for one another to weather the storm.

Take a hypothetical scenario. The primary breadwinner of a couple loses his or her job. All of a sudden, the family income is at best dramatically decreased and at worst gone all together.

Now let's imagine the scenario happens to two different couples. The first couple has a solid relationship. Sure, there's arguing. Sure, each has annoyances with the other. But by and large, the pair operates as a team. If you were to ask either of them about the overall state of their relationship, you would find that they are both satisfied. That they have love and respect for each other. And that they've shared many good times together.

The second couple is constantly bickering and putting each other down. Long before the job loss, there were issues: One felt taken for granted, the other felt ignored. They hadn't had any fun together in years. Instead of operating as a team, they essentially coexist, cohabitate, coparent.

Which couple is more likely to come out of something as serious as a job loss and major financial blow intact?

How couples communicate with each other isn't just essential to the health of their own relationship, but the one that they have with their children as well. Gottman said the same patterns in the way a couple speaks to each other are replicated in the parent-child relationship.

"Criticism of a partner as a character flaw," he said, "will be applied to the child as well." He said using phrases like "you're lazy," or "you always" or "you never" are common in marriage and then repeat themselves with children.

"People tend to look around for other people's mistakes to explain their own bad mood," Gottman said.

Well that certainly rang true. Good mood = nice Genny, patient Genny, loving Genny. Bad/stressed mood = critical Genny, yelling Genny, irritable Genny.

Happy people, he said, instead look around for things to appreciate, not things to criticize. Getting into this pattern with a spouse will eventually lead to interacting with kids the same way.

It's not easy, he said. "Communicating with another person is as hard as operating a 747," Gottman told me. "People think it should be easy. That's just not true."

Even mothers and babies, he said, are miscoordinated in their communication with each other about 70 percent of the time.

Ryan and I found that much of the time spent together after the kids were (finally) asleep was spent organizing our calendars, discussing what was upcoming with the children, rehashing the conversation one of us had had with the mortgage broker/therapist/preschool teacher, etc. So we devised a plan where we'd talk during the workday instead. And most weekdays, usually around midafternoon, my desk phone rings with a familiar number and I smile.

"Hi, I just wanted to check in," he says. And then we spend anywhere between five and ten minutes tending to the "business" of parenthood.

Since I rarely leave my desk for more than a bathroom break or a trip to the office refrigerator to retrieve my lunch all day long, I'm not worried about the calls. And if something is pressing at work at the moment the phone rings, I just tell Ryan it's not a good time to talk and that's that. Ryan's got a very busy job, too, and he gets it. There're no hard feelings.

But on most days, there's enough time to talk through the work of being parents—the schedules, the parent-teacher conference sign-ups, the forms that need to be signed. And when we can get those conversations out of the way during the day, it allows us time at home to just be. To talk about something funny one of the kids said or to make fun of something on television. Whatever it was, it was easier to relax and laugh knowing the details were taken care of.

For a while, we tried to meet for lunch once a week, too. But as it turned out, finding a time that we could each leave the office for an hour-plus was very challenging. And sometimes the lunch would be stressful, because one or both of us was worried about the work piling up or the meeting we were cutting it close for.

And while there are certain disagreements and a certain level of bickering that will take place in front of the kids, there are some things they just can't witness.

It's those moments—the ones that are going to put your life on one course or another; the ones when your life or marriage is at a crossroads—when the troops must be called in. Whether that's family, friends, neighbors, and whatever the particular situation you find yourselves in is, you'll know the moment. And adult problems are not ever appropriate for children to witness. Further, adult conversations simply cannot take place when young kids who have no understanding of anyone's needs but their own will not allow meaningful conversation, and hopefully resolution, to take place.

But those moments, thankfully, are generally few and far between. Far more commonplace is quiet dissatisfaction with marriage, with life, that eventually seems to lead to not only marital unhappiness but also an overall unhappiness.

There's research to suggest that the happiness of the woman in the relationship—so, the moms, for the readers of this book—is of particular importance to the overall happiness in a marriage. In other words *happy wife, happy life* is actually true.

In a September 12, 2014, article on *Rutgers Today*, the university's news website, the following reports on a recent study:

"I think it comes down to the fact that when a wife is satisfied with the marriage, she tends to do a lot more for her husband, which has a positive effect on his life," said Deborah Carr, a professor in the Department of Sociology, at Rutgers' School of Arts and Science. "Men tend to be less vocal about their relationships and their level of marital unhappiness might not be translated to their wives."

Deborah Carr and Vicki Freedman, a research professor at the University of Michigan Institute for Social Research, coauthored a research study published in the October issue of the *Journal of Marriage and Family* on marital quality and happiness among older adults.

The study, "Happy Marriage, Happy Life? Marital Quality and Subjective Well-being in Later Life," done by the two Big Ten universities, differs from previous research, according to Carr, because it examines the personal feelings of both spouses to determine how these marital appraisals influence the psychological well-being of older adults. Researchers analyzed data of 394 couples who were part of a national study of income, health, and disability in 2009. At least one of the spouses was sixty or older and, on average, couples had been married for thirty-nine years.

In order to assess marital quality, those involved in the study were asked several questions, such as whether their spouse appreciates them, argues with them, understands their feelings, or gets on their nerves. They were also asked to keep detailed diaries about how happy they were in the previous twenty-four hours doing selected activities such as shopping and household chores and watching television.

Those involved in the study, on average, rated their general life satisfaction high, typically 5 out of 6 points.

"For both spouses, being in a better-rated marriage was linked to greater life satisfaction and happiness," Carr said.

There's no shortage of marriage counselors out there, but how do you know when you really need one? And how do you know when the issues in your marriage are actual marriage issues, and not your own personal stuff you need to deal with?

I don't pretend to have the answer. But I do have a feeling that the day-to-day annoyances that turn into bigger issues over time might be avoided by changing our own behavior, letting our needs be known, extending common courtesy, and choosing to shut up instead of talking more often than not.

I know that sounds a little harsh. We live in a society that seems to reward people who speak their minds at any cost. But I think in a marriage, it makes a lot of sense to keep roughly 90 percent of what you'd like to say in. First: the vast majority of things said in anger are just that, and serve no purpose except to hurt. Second, when we're constantly nagging or complaining, our words not only annoy but lose their impact. So when there is something we need to say that actually matters, it risks getting lost in all the other noise we've created.

Most of the little arguments Ryan and I have are of the "who is doing more" variety. I work, he works. I'm tired, he's tired. He is a hands-on dad, I am a hands-on mom. Suffice to say that we're both doing the best we can.

But there are weeks that seem totally off balance. Weeks where it feels like he's skating by and I'm in the trenches.

Those are the weeks when keeping quiet proves challenging. Recently, a confluence of events totally out of anyone's control left me largely on my own for a week: Ryan had a three-hour postwork board meeting for GiGi's Playhouse NYC, a Down syndrome achievement center. Another night he had a work-related dinner with a potential client, who, if he came on board, would make a significant financial difference in our lives. Plus two nights spent in Boston, visiting with his father who was having surgery for gallstones. And finally, drinks with a dear friend who was celebrating his birthday.

Only one of those events sounded like any fun whatsoever of course. But still, I was irate. So I had a week of mornings and then nights on my own, with my only "break" being work.

But luckily, I saw a sign. An actual, physical sign. It hangs in my apartment. It's called The Brown Family Rules and it was purchased for the kids to remind them what's expected of them. And for the two years that sign has been staring me in the face, it never occurred to me that the rules set forth—by us, the parents who created the sign—were not always being followed by the grown-ups in the home but were absolutely expected to be adhered to by two toddlers. Because that makes sense.

The Brown Family Rules

Be kind
Be grateful
Be nice to others
Be proud
Say please
Say thank you
Keep your promises
Listen to each other
Tell the truth
Say I love you
Laugh
Know how much you are loved

I had a lot of these nailed, at least outside of my own marriage. I could definitely be a little more grateful toward Ryan. I could definitely stand to say please and thank you more.

But the one that stuck out to me somehow is "know how much you are loved." Because that week, deep in the trenches, Ryan nowhere to be found, I was definitely not feeling loved.

It was a sentiment I should express more in order to make Ryan feel more loved, and it was something I could benefit from feeling, too. Think about it for a minute. Do you ever stop to consider how much your spouse must love you in order to have decided to spend his life with you? My love for Ryan feels so natural, so strong. Every day, every decision I make, everything I do—I am thinking about him. But does he know that? Does he know how much I worry about his happiness? How much I wonder if I'm enough? How sometimes I think that he sold himself short by marrying me—that he could have done much better?

Certainly, he could have married someone easier. That's actually something we've joked about in the past. He had a tendency to date people pleasers before he dated me. Or, at the very least, people who didn't rock the proverbial boat much. But then, for some reason, he inexplicably chose me.

Of all the things I am—loyal, hardworking, quick to laugh, optimistic—there is one thing I'm not. And that's easy. No one in my life would ever say that their relationship with me is an easy one. And since no one is closer to me than Ryan, it stands to reason that out of all the people whose lives I make more difficult simply by being in it, I make his the most difficult.

Because those positive traits I listed are just as easily countered by not-so-positive ones: inflexible, emotional, impatient, and demanding.

And yet. He's still here. It doesn't appear that he has any desire to be anywhere else. Is it possible that despite all my crazy, he loves me just as much as I love him? That the decisions he makes every day are made with me in mind? That he worries about my happiness, too?

If I accept this, and frame our interactions with that belief in mind, what happens?

I decided to try. And once I did, and stopped looking for things to criticize and started looking for things to appreciate, as Gottman suggested, there was a lot less tension, especially in those crazy morning hours. Because I began to notice how Ryan loaded the dishwasher every night after I went to bed, how he arranged for the laundry to be picked up each week, how he would often cook a big meal each Sunday so I wouldn't have to worry about what we were going to eat a couple nights that week, how he always had me choose what kind of takeout to get when it was an order-in night.

How he treated our children with the same love he treated me. How he was the one who found, purchased tickets for, and took Will to the *The Gazillion Bubble Show*, his first live performance, which captivated him. How he made sure our zoo membership never expired and often took the children to see and feed the animals, even if he forgot to wash their hands after. How he had "movie night" dates with Addie several times a month where he made popcorn because even though she doesn't eat popcorn, she really likes making it. How he was frequently the only dad willing to hop in the pool for their back-to-back swim lessons with all the moms while I watched from the stands.

I could go on and on.

When you simply know and accept how much you—and your children—are loved by your spouse, criticism is a lot harder to dole out, and gratitude that much easier. It's a recipe for a Happy Mommy, indeed.

Chapter 6

Take Yourself to the Doctor

Moms Need Checkups, Too

I was on a vacation with my husband's family, and my sister-in-law was bringing me up to speed on some friends of hers I know peripherally. She mentioned Lara, a lovely woman I haven't seen since my sister-in-law's wedding nearly eight years ago. Although I don't know Lara well at all, she has three kids and a high-powered, big-city job—basically, she's who I want to be when I grow up—and I'm always eager to hear what she's been up to.

"Oh, Lara—well, she's OK. But she has thyroid cancer. So of course I'm worried about her."

"Thyroid cancer?" I said. "That's terrible. Is she going to be OK?"

"I think so," my sister-in-law said. "She's got a really good attitude about it, very positive."

"How long has she had it?" I asked.

"See, that's the thing," said Kerry. "She's not exactly sure. Maybe awhile, but she just found out."

"What do you mean?"

"You know, she was just feeling so incredibly tired and run down, not herself at all. But she never went to the doctor because she thought that was normal. She just figured that was what you were supposed to feel like when you have three kids, so it took her a really long time to see anyone."

"Let me get this straight," I said. "She had cancer—actual cancer—and she mistook it for the same kind of exhaustion that comes from being a parent?"

"Yep."

I was stunned. I was also very glad to hear Lara's prognosis was positive. But the fact that a person could have cancer—actual real-life cancer—and chalk up how they were feeling to parenting really shook me to my core.

Because you know what? I could totally see how that would happen. And that's terrifying.

The Paradox of Mommy Health

Since Addie was born, I go to the doctor. A lot.

There are those first few pediatrician appointments that come right after the baby's born. Three day, one week, one month, three month, six month, one year, eighteen months, two years. That's assuming nothing out of the ordinary is happening.

Because there are also the trips for the coughing. The rash. The runny nose that won't quit.

And then if you have a child with special needs, which I do, there's a hell of a lot more. For Will, it's the ENT—checkups, hearing tests, and three surgeries so far. He also sees an endocrinologist every six months to check his thyroid. Then we see a Down syndrome specialist every six months to check in on his progress.

Last fall was particularly filled with doctor's visits. Will had his two-year-old well visit with his pediatrician and then afterward promptly came down with a cold. So it was back to the doctor, who said she suspected it was viral and there was little to do but wait it out.

It so happened that he was already scheduled to visit a different doctor in Boston a few weeks later, for a hearing test and ear tube surgery (his second such surgery in two years). So my husband and I took off two days from work and booked a Boston hotel room. My mom stayed with Addie in New York while we were away.

First up: Will's hearing test. It's been an ongoing issue for him since birth, and we've made many trips to Boston to meet with this special ear doctor about his various issues. Only one parent was allowed in the hearing test room, and that parent was me. I could immediately tell it wasn't going well. As I heard the tones the tester was playing and discerned by Will's nonreactions that he didn't, my anxiety level was going off the charts.

By the time we walked out of the testing room, I was a mess. I asked the tester to tell me what she thought, how bad was it, really? In my mind, what I was really concerned about was how long this had been going on without my knowing.

Ryan and I will often spot-check Will's hearing on our own. You know, stand across the room, say his name in various volumes, and see his reaction. We also pay special attention to his reaction to noises outside the window or inside the apartment. And truthfully, things had seemed pretty good from our perspective. The only reason I was so sure he would be having the ear tube surgery at all was because I know his doctor, who is pretty aggressive, and I knew he would think they would only do him good.

And now I was terrified that I had been very, very wrong. That I had somehow misread all those "tests" and that he hadn't been hearing anything we were saying at all. And that it would lead to an even larger speech delay than the one we were currently experiencing. And it was all my fault. I felt I had failed my child, and the guilt, coupled with complete panic, was overwhelming.

We went to see the doctor, who indeed confirmed that Will's hearing was far worse than it had been after his last hearing test, when it had been very close to perfect. He checked Will's ears and could see one tube, but not the other. Yes, he definitely needed the surgery.

"But," he said, "I can't operate on him tomorrow as planned. With his congestion, it's not safe to put him under anesthesia. I'm giving him antibiotics, for two weeks, and then he should be clear enough to operate."

Of course the second I heard the words "not safe," the surgery was off the table. I had already watched Will be put under anesthesia twice before, and it was scary enough without any outstanding issues. But I couldn't help but be a little irritated that we had come all this way. Only to be turned away.

Despite my frustration with the futility of this particular trip, the truth is I never hesitate to rework my schedule or jump through hoops to see the right doctor when my children need medical care. Neither do you, I'm sure. We're parents. That's just what we do. I estimate that in the three years since I had become a mom, I have made a minimum of forty-five trips to various doctors.

And excluding the appointments related to pregnancy, I have been to the doctor—for myself—a total of zero times.

Zero.

Talk about parents putting ourselves last. Literally, our most important job is to be there, be present, and be healthy for our children. And yet most of us are almost pathological about avoiding the medical care that will enable us to do this most vital of jobs for our families.

To be fair, I consider myself to be in very good health. I rarely get even a cold, and when I do, it's of the variety that I know is not worth seeing a doctor about because it'll be gone in a few days on its own. Thankfully, I don't have any chronic diseases that I'm leaving unattended. In some ways, I'm actually healthier than I was before I became a mom: I used to get seasonal allergies, but these disappeared when I was pregnant with Addie and never came back.

But there's something else that I got when I was pregnant with Addie that's been bothering me for three and a half years. It's a pain in the middle of my back, a pain that on some days is so unbearable I can't sit still and on others, so bad I can't sleep at night.

I have not been to a doctor to check this out. In more than three years.

I'm fairly certain the pain is from two things: carrying my bag to and from work over the same shoulder, and lifting and holding the kids—especially Will, who loves nothing more than to be carried around, especially in his fussy evening hours. The reason I am pretty sure this is the case is that when I'm away from work and the kids, even just for two days, the pain all but fades away.

Still, it's a little disturbing for others—Ryan, namely, the only person who really sees my unclothed back—to look at. There is a visible bulge next to my spine on the right side in the middle of my back.

"You really, really need to get that looked at," he's said several times.

It's ironic, really. Up until a few years ago, Ryan had not been to a doctor since he went to his pediatrician for his off-to-college physical. But there came a point when he was complaining of migraines and I insisted he see someone. He resisted. I would not relent. He eventually did go and was given medication that helped him tremendously. After that, he was a convert. He went to a sports medicine doctor for a foot injury. He got a weird-looking bug bite and went to the doctor only to find out it was Lyme disease (he is fine now). When he gets a bad cold? He walks a few blocks from our apartment to the twenty-four-hour, no-appointment-required City MD for antibiotics.

He goes to the doctor because of me, and I orchestrate my kids' regular visits. Yet I never see a doctor, despite this bulge in my back.

Judging from the complaints of other mothers I know, back pain seems like it's par for the course when it comes to raising kids. There's the constant lifting, the bending over about one hundred times a day, the carrying of a giant bag filled with their "necessities" every place you go, the pushing of a double stroller that, in my case, weighs a minimum of 100 pounds (stroller itself and seats: 35 pounds; Addie, 40 pounds; Will, 25 pounds)—and that's without anything extra, like a week's worth of groceries, in it.

But ignoring pain can have serious consequences. According to the American Chiropractic Association (ACA), it's one of the most common reasons for missing work. Missing work at any job is certainly frowned upon; missing work at my office is career suicide.

A study by the ACA of more than two thousand people who suffer from back pain found it had all sorts of ramifications in their daily lives. More than one-third said it made them more irritable; almost 20 percent said it led to a decrease in participation in hobbies; 8 percent said it made it impossible to look after their children.

Check, check and going down that path.

Ignoring their own health and yet obsessing over the health of their children seems to be a problem moms pass down through the ages. At least in my family. My own mother, now in her seventies, gets visibly annoyed if someone suggests she go to a doctor to find out why xyz is bothering her. And yet she gets equally annoyed at me when I ignore her "suggestions" (they sound more like orders) to go to the doctor when I'm under the weather. At the center of all this illness-ignoring/going-to-the-doctor-avoiding is the issue of time. There's just "no time" to see a doctor, according to my mother, myself, and every other mother I know. If we (moms) take the time to go to the doctor, who is going to take the kids to the playdate, attend the meeting at work, meet with the pre-K teacher about this quarter's evaluation?

And yet I've been known to push off a deadline or take a half day in order to make sure Addie or Will gets to the doctor. I have never missed one of their doctor appointments, no matter what else was going on in life. There's nothing more important than their health, I tell myself. But literally everything seems to be more important than mine, and every other mom I know.

Paging Dr. Google

The weeks following the canceled ear tube surgery—the one I had taken two days off of work for—brought many more doctors' appointments, though none of them mine. The antibiotics Will was prescribed seemed at first to be getting the job done, but then I thought he seemed to be taking a turn for the worse, so back to the pediatrician we went. Again, she said it was viral and gave no medication. This sick visit required a ninety-minute break in the middle of my workday.

The very next week, Addie said her throat bothered her. So though she had no temperature and seemed otherwise fine, I arrived at her school midday, signed her out, and we took a taxi to the pediatrician, where we found out she did, in fact, have strep throat, and she was prescribed antibiotics.

Addie's illness occurred just before I made her annual well-visit appointment. Because I really couldn't justify another break in the middle of the day, I made the appointment for 8 p.m. on a Tuesday—the only one left on the one night a month the doctor (who is a working parent herself) works late to accommodate working parents.

Then I decided that the doctor was wrong and Will's illness was not viral. And even if it was, I was going to get her to prescribe him something anyway, because I was at the end of my rope watching him suffer. Swollen, tired eyes; disrupted sleep; irritated nose from constant wiping. This is not something a mom can sit by and watch.

While I waited for yet the next appointment to go back to the same doctor to deal with Will's congestion, I consulted Dr. Google on possible alternative remedies. Because obviously moms—who are not busy enough—have time in their "downtime" to educate themselves on the benefits of alternative medicine while they wait for actual doctors to help their children feel better. The ones we pay for this service.

It was a mix of desperation and rage that had me ordering $100 of essential oils from Amazon on the same day I found a chiropractor who claimed to be able to help kids with chronic congestion. It was a Thursday, and I emailed her office to see if she could see Will the following day. She could not, but she did have an opening that afternoon at 3:45. Or it could wait until Monday morning. I'll give you one guess which one I picked.

It was 3 p.m. I work on the Upper West Side. I had to pick up Will on the Upper East Side and then get to midtown, all in the next forty-five minutes. I told the doctor I would be there, shut down my computer, raced across town in a cab, got Will in his stroller, and walked the mile with him to the chiropractor's office.

She said she could feel that his neck and one part of his

upper back were very stiff—likely, she said, due to his chronic congestion. It seemed to be months of buildup, she said. She educated me on the importance of opening the neck and spine so that everything has the ability to flow through.

Yeah, yeah, yeah, I thought the whole time. *Are you going to help my kid feel better or not? I've got places to be.*

She performed a slight adjustment on Will, which he didn't seem to mind, though he did visibly react when she touched the places she mentioned were blocked up. It made me happy because I felt that what she was saying might be legit. She warned me that night might be the worst I had seen so far in terms of runny nose, and it was. But then she noticed I was hunched over a bit, and she asked me how I was feeling.

"Pretty good," I said. "You know, fine."

She looked at me quizzically.

"Oh," I said. "Well, I mean, I have a lot of back pain. But that's nothing new." I added, "It's actually been like four years."

"Four years? That's a sign of a real problem. Why don't you make an appointment to come see me, too, and let's see if I can help you feel better."

Big pause. The chiropractor doesn't take insurance. And while I had no problem forking over $185 for Will's first appointment and $85 for each appointment thereafter (and I had just scheduled a series of weekly appointments for him), it seemed excessive when it came to me.

It's so hypocritical, isn't it? The way moms use vacation days, schedule dozens of appointments for their kids, repeating the mantra that nothing is more important than their kids' health, all the while completely ignoring their own? I thought about my ongoing project to put myself first once in a while and treat myself with the same care and attention I lavish on my kids every day.

And then I left, without making an appointment for myself. After all, I was just too busy.

Meanwhile, the essential oils I had ordered for Will did not seem to be making a difference, but that didn't stop me from adding lavender oil to both kids' baths each night and putting something called myrtle into the humidifier in their room before they drifted off to sleep. (Yes, they were both still getting the spa treatment. What can I say, I love my sleep . . . and my sleep is still inextricably tied to their sleep!) I had high hopes for the myrtle—the research I conducted on the holistic medicine mommy boards led me to believe that it was all but a miracle cure for blocked sinuses.

And several mornings in a row, when I heard Will stir, I ran into his room, expecting the myrtle would have cured his congestion. No dice.

During this flurry of appointments and my stint as a holistic medicine doctor, I too developed some sort of cold. It started out with some sneezing, and then a stuffy nose, and then merged into a full-blown cough that kept me up half the night. I had a headache every day for two weeks and generally felt like garbage. But I could not see a doctor or take a day off—because I had already spent the last three weeks doing that for my kids. And now there was no wiggle room left.

Funny, I never tried the myrtle on myself.

And that back pain wasn't getting any better.

Meanwhile, Ryan and I have become so close with one of Will's doctors that we've agreed to fund-raise for him. It's a worthy cause, no doubt, and one I'm happy to commit to because it's so close to my heart. But when I take a step back and look at my life from an outsider's point of view, it would seem insane to commit myself to planning and hosting fund-raisers for *other* doctors and patients . . . when I can't even take care of my basic needs.

Of course this could be said of many things I do instead of seeing a doctor. Getting my hair done? That's three hours every few months. Nail appointments? At least ninety minutes every few weeks.

The fact is that my health has just not been a priority. I do think part of the issue is doctor overload. My kids have few health issues and yet I am completely sick of doctor's appointments, insurance issues, and, frankly, the nagging feeling that more than a few of them don't really know what they're talking about anyway.

My cold is one thing. I know it's going to go away on its own, eventually. Maybe it would go away faster if I saw a doctor. Maybe not. The back pain, though—I'm pretty sure it's not serious, but who knows until you've seen someone?

Sometimes I think about what would happen to my kids if I died. It breaks my heart to think of them growing up without me, without the daily hugs and kisses, without hearing me tell them how much I love them day in and day out.

So why am I neglecting my own most basic needs?

Taking Control of My Own Health, at Last

Here's the question I have to ask myself: When Addie and Will are adults, and if one of them is in a varying degree of pain literally every day as I am yet has never reached out to a doctor, what would I do?

I would drag them to the doctor myself. And I would not take no for an answer.

With that level of conviction in mind, I decide I can't put it off anymore.

This behavior of mine does not a good mother make, I decided right then and there. Because if I don't take care of myself, and I find myself in a situation where I've ignored something to the point of it putting me with those 8 percent of people who said their back pain rendered them incapable of taking care of their kids, then I actually am a crappy mother.

I made my own chiropractor appointment for a few days later. And when I came in, the doctor was visibly surprised when she examined my back.

"This is not at all subtle," she said, referring to the bulging muscle in my midback. "This feels more like a bone than a muscle at this point."

OK, lady, I've got places to be, I thought. *Let's get this fixed up so I can be on my way.*

"I'm actually surprised you've been able to function like this," she went on. "You're on the verge of a serious injury."

I started to get the feeling this wasn't going to be a one-shot deal.

"You're only going to be lifting more and have even less time as these kids get older," she said. "I think you need to come at least twice a week."

How in the hell was I going to find time to come twice a week?

She went on to tell me about patients—all moms—who had ignored their pain to the point of being part of that 8 percent. In one case, she told me about a mom who had just given birth to her third and became physically incapable of picking up even her newborn.

"And unlike you," she said, "she didn't even have to worry about having a job to go to."

This is not to in any way say that the health of a working mom trumps that of a stay-at-home mom. But the doctor did have a point. If I could not report to work due to back pain, we were going to have problems a lot more serious than the current discomfort I was experiencing.

Still, the time commitment—and the price tag—was a lot. So I decided to compromise, and made an appointment for the following week. I had already scheduled an appointment for Will, so I would be seeing the doc twice anyway.

Dr. Karen Erickson, a practicing chiropractor who sees moms and kids and is also a spokesperson for the American Chiropractic Association, told me that the physiological changes a woman experiences during pregnancy and after can actually cause her body to misalign more easily. Which means that I was not at all alone in my seemingly chronic back pain.

Breast-feeding, bottle-feeding, pushing strollers, carrying diaper bags and babies who get heavier every day—all of it adds up to strain on the body that people who are not mothers—or at least not a child's primary caretaker—simply don't have to deal with.

"Moms essentially become human mules," she said.

I laughed out loud when she said it. Because my father has called my mother, whose first name is Maita, "Maita the mule" for as long as I can remember. She is literally always carrying something from here to there. There's nothing too heavy for her, even now that she is a seven-time grandmother. It's a trait I've inherited, and Ryan often calls me "the ant," a reference to the fact that ants carry up to five thousand times their body weight.

And this back pain that is so common, Erickson said, tends to get worse as babies become toddlers. Simultaneously, their schedule starts to drive yours, making it more and more complicated to actually schedule the time to have any health ailments checked out.

While health issues affect women across all economic brackets, of course, getting to the doctor is particularly difficult for women who are financially unable to hire a babysitter to take care of their children while they see a doctor for themselves. And so health issues—their own—get ignored.

I realized when she said it that I was far better off than so many other women, at least in that regard. I had the means and the access to attend to my health. I had decent health insurance, something so many people in our country lack. What I didn't have, the thing I kept harping on, was the time. But when I took a moment to really think about it, so much of my lack of time was by my own design. I was often resentful of how busy I was, and yet I did nothing—nothing—to free up some time.

Erickson said the consequences of a mother neglecting her health went deeper than the ailment itself.

Ignoring the signals your body is giving you teaches your kids to do the same thing. What mothers should be doing, at least to the extent they can, Erickson said, is showing their kids that the "reasonable thing to do is to try and take care of it." Good health allows us to further enjoy the experience of parenting.

I can't help but think about my own mother once more. She may be the perfect woman. I'm serious about it—you can ask anyone who knows her. She is kind, thoughtful, generous, loving, supportive. But she's never been attentive to her own health. Luckily, she's generally quite healthy. But when she isn't, she won't see a doctor. And she has to be all but incapacitated to even slow down. She takes care of our kids twice each week and on only one occasion did she "call in sick." (And that was only because she was worried about the children.) If there was no chance of her infecting the kids, I can assure you she would be vomiting in a paper bag in between school pickup, art class drop-off, and never-ending rounds of "here comes Thumbkin."

As Erickson reminded me, moms never get a break. "From the moment you wake up in the morning, you are on," she said.

Apparently this "on-ness" extends well into grandparent-hood, at least for some.

It occurred to me, too, that moms are actually "on" all night, too. A child wakes up from a nightmare, or to go to the bathroom, or because they can't find their lovey—and there's only one person they want to fix it: Mom.

When the physical and emotional demands of a job—in this case motherhood—go on literally twenty-four hours every day, there is no chance to recover, Erickson said.

"But there is real power in acknowledging that sometimes you can't do what you have to do to take care of yourself," she added. "Just being conscious of it—the pain or the sleep deprivation—can be powerful. So you wake up from a terrible night's sleep with a day's worth of activities ahead. What can you do? Maybe you can't sleep more. But maybe you can take a few minutes to meditate or make a plan to get to bed early that night."

Parenting, Erickson told me, is a "spiritual journey. Your children polish your soul and show you your rough edges. They teach you to embrace your humanness."

After taking some time to reflect on that statement, I think I know what she meant. Because in the day-to-day, I can't say being a mom feels very spiritual at all, though when I find myself thanking God for anything, it is always my kids. But when I imagine a spiritual journey, I am always by myself, ten pounds thinner, doing yoga, rested and relaxed, and most often getting a massage.

I'm never, ever cleaning poop out of a bathtub. There's no snot on my shoulder.

And yet, I realize that my children have indeed polished my soul. Addie changed me the day she was born, teaching me what true, unconditional love felt like. Not to receive, but to give. And Will showed me how to be brave. My big personality often masked my deepest feelings of insecurity. But now, because of him, I'm no longer scared. It's amazingly liberating after spending thirty years worried about what other people think of me, to no longer give it a second thought.

I'm a much better version of me, because of them. Albeit a more tired one.

"We do ourselves a disservice," Erickson said, "acting like we have it together all the time."

Agreed. We all need a person or two we can fall apart in front of from time to time. But I do think there is some truth to the saying "Fake it till you make it." Because when there's so much to do in any given day, what does it help to fall apart? Isn't it sometimes easier just to keep on going? To put one foot in front of another until you've checked off everything on the to-do list?

For me, the answer is yes. And so I continued my weekly chiropractor visits—for both me and Will—and scheduled his ear tube surgery for the third time. I took more time off of work, booked another hotel room, arranged for my mom to stay overnight with Addie—and Ryan and I headed back up to Boston.

Will had caught yet another cold in the one week he had been off antibiotics before our arrival. But his ENT didn't feel it was bad enough to cancel the surgery. And in our pre-operation clearance meeting, he offered us another theory of what might be going on.

"I think it could be his adenoids. If they're infected, it would make sense that the antibiotics work to clear up most of the infection, but not all. And then as soon as the antibiotics are done, the bacteria that's so far back in the adenoids just starts growing again, and he gets sick."

He suggested that during the surgery, in addition to the ear tubes, he remove Will's adenoids.

Adenoids, as it turns out, don't serve much of a purpose. Adults actually don't even have them. But if infected, they can cause chronic sinus problems in kids, as well as sleep issues.

Let's get rid of them, we decided.

The doctor told us that Will would be under anesthesia, which was always the case with ear tubes, but that he would be put into a deeper sleep, one that would require a breathing tube during the operation. No parent wants to hear the words "breathing tube" in a conversation about their beloved child, but we trusted Will's ENT who would perform the surgery, and knew he trusted the anesthesiologist.

Soon, a nurse came out to tell us Will's surgery was over, and he was starting to wake up from the anesthesia. I practically ran to the recovery room, where a woman I didn't know sat rocking him in a chair. He was screaming at the top of his lungs, not an uncommon reaction for someone coming out of anesthesia, but a very unusual state for our normally very happy toddler.

I held him for a while until he calmed, and eventually we were released from the hospital. The three of us started the three-hour drive from Boston to New York, Ryan and I so hopeful that this was the answer—that the operation would provide Will the relief from his chronic congestion and Ryan and I from the constant worry, Internet searching, doctor-appointment making, and holistic remedy-seeking path we had been headed down for the last nine months.

It took ten days, but it worked. It was unsettling that things got worse before they got better, but the doctors had prepared us.

As it turned out, the chiropractor wasn't ever going to be able to "fix" Will's congestion. That's not to say that there aren't other benefits for children to visit a chiropractor, or to say that I wouldn't take him back. It was a close-to-$1,000 error on my part, not to mention the time of getting to and from the appointments that were never going to clear from his adenoids an infection so deep that surgery was the only cure.

But those appointments, originally intended for Will, did end up forcing me to address a problem I had had for years. My back issue is not yet resolved, but it would be foolish to think an ailment four years in the making could be cured in a few twenty-minute sessions.

I have no idea if the chiropractor is the long-term answer to my chronic back pain. I know now, though, that even with all the appointments I make for the kids, I can also squeeze myself in. What once would have seemed logistically impossible—a weekly appointment for myself to address a health issue—actually turned out to be one of the more pleasant parts of my week, once I figured out the day and time that worked—Wednesdays at 8:30 a.m., right after I dropped Addie off and before I went to work.

And if the chiropractor turns out not to be the answer, now I'll keep looking, knowing that taking care of myself is not only critical but doable, even with a schedule that seems impossibly tight. Like the rest of motherhood, it's a matter of juggling, a matter of logistics, a matter of scheduling.

But unlike many of the other things we moms busy ourselves with—arts and crafts, playdate scheduling, and creating Pinterest-worthy lunchboxes—letting our own health slip through the cracks has detrimental effects. Because if Mom is laid up in bed or worse, there will be no one left to do those arts and crafts anyway.

Move It

*Exercise Even If You Don't Have
the Time, Money, or Interest*

||'m going to run the marathon next year."

Often, declarations made after several drinks are ones
we regret the next morning. In this case, though, those words
I said in a bar, on Marathon Sunday 2014, were the gateway
to what has become the single most important thing I'm now
doing for myself. This is one area that, surprisingly, I didn't
have to work as hard at to put myself first. I was ready, willing, and eager to schedule the time into my busy schedule
to commit to running a big race. But life, it turned out, had
other plans.

My relationship with physical fitness is like the one you had
with your high school boyfriend. In high school, it was fine.
The relationship was fun and easy. You had mutual friends.
And then you went away to college and it became harder
to maintain, as there were so many distractions. Eventually,
your contact lessened, and you were only seeing each other
a few times a year, and mostly in the summer. Once you left

your parents' house to move to the city, you rarely saw each other at all.

But a few times a year, you were reunited for whatever reason—maybe the wedding of a friend—and you hung out, and had fun, and it felt great, and you wondered why you let so much time pass between times seeing this person who was once such a big part of your life and you were still fond of.

This was me with exercise: the captain of the high school swim team now diminished into a few attempts a year to "get back into it."

My shrinking interest in fitness is not unique. For one thing, gyms are expensive. They are a luxury for most of us. It's also hard to carve out the time to make it to a class regularly, I know. (See: getting to the doctor, in the previous chapter.) But as it turns out, the various fitness opportunities for us moms are not as expensive—or time consuming—as the "fitness" classes or sports leagues many of us have our children enrolled in.

Adelaide has been enrolled in four semesters of Super Soccer Stars, two semesters of swimming lessons, one session of ballet, one class at Jodi's Gym, a playgroup at Kidville gym, and two rounds of T-ball. (These are only the classes that are based primarily on physical activity; she's been in many others, too.)

Before I became a mom, I did splurge on fitness sometimes. On the corner of Madison Avenue and 77th Street, near my house, is Exhale. Exhale is a spa that also offers fitness classes. Its signature class is a barre class called Core Fusion. It's sixty minutes of body-shaping torture with a list of devotees so long that there's often a waiting list for classes. When I first started going to Exhale, I had no business being there (and by that I mean that I was in fine physical shape, but not in a financial position to be treating myself to $50-an-hour workout classes). There are far less expensive fitness options, of course, and at that time, I had no kids and was bound by pretty much nothing except money.

But I loved the class, and so I kept going. I even went in the early part of my pregnancy with Adelaide, up until the point where a core workout just became silly. I had no visible core—just a round ball where the core used to be. So I stuck to running instead.

Sometime after my daughter was born, Ryan (at my request) gifted to me a twenty-pack of Core Fusion classes at the Exhale spa that is literally on our street. I have gone to two so far.

That's two classes—in three years.

Each morning on my way to the ABC offices, I take the same route, which involves walking past Exhale. Each morning I hear the class in progress. I hear the instructor counting down from ten and I imagine the people in the class standing at the barre, exercise ball pressed between their knees as they squat through the burning pain and pray for the torture to end.

God I miss that class.

There's a pang of regret each morning, not only for missing out on something I love but also for the hundreds of dollars in classes that are just going to waste.

At the time I was a Core Fusion devotee, I had all the time in the world and very limited money. Now I can more easily afford the class, but I can't for the life of me figure out a time to go. And the truth is, Ryan has on at least ten separate occasions asked me to simply pick a day of the week I'd like to go, and he will see that the kids get up and ready so I can go to an early class. So what's stopping me? Is it the guilt of taking time away from the kids? Is it guilt for putting the responsibility of child care on Ryan on an additional morning (he already does quite a bit)? Is it worry that, without me, the whole morning will fall apart?

All of the above.

Mile by Mile

Which brings me to that bar, on Marathon Sunday, and my (slightly tipsy) proclamations: "I'm going to run the marathon next year."

I wish the NY Road Runners, the race's organizers, had some sort of app where drunken marathon watchers could go, moved by inspiration, and immediately register to run this incredible race the following year. Participation would soar.

Some people would wake up the next morning and not give their pledge another thought, of course. But I make a point of following through on what I say I am going to do (and besides, this could be the way to get back into fitness and prioritize my own health as a mom). Easy peasy. I'm really getting the hang of this Happiest Mommy stuff, eh?

And that's how I came to get back into running and secured myself a spot in the 2015 New York City Marathon, running for LuMind Research Down Syndrome Foundation, an organization that raises money to fund research for the improvement of cognition in people with Down syndrome.

Of all the people in my life who inspire me—primarily my parents and my husband and children—there is no one who inspires me more than my son. A person who will face challenges in life I've never had to consider because of an extra chromosome. A person who, at two years old, has changed us all for the better. A person who smiles through nine therapy sessions—a combination of PT, OT and speech—a week. A person whose smile and belly laugh lights up a room.

A person who—since he was just weeks old—has endured three one-hour physical therapy sessions per week. We call it baby exercise. If my little toddler can get his baby exercise, and endure it with such joy and love—and if my exercise can in some way support him?—well, sign me up.

Ryan was aghast when I announced my marathon plans. "You don't have time to train," he said. What a buzzkill.

My mother offered similar nonsupport. "Gen, you already have too much on your plate. How are you going to do this?" Ouch.

Their words stung, as words with at least some truth to them often do. After I secured my number, I got scared. Now it was real. Mind you, I wasn't exactly a rookie at this running stuff. I've jogged off and on for years, and I have run the marathon once before—in 2007, prior to having kids. So I knew exactly how much time and effort goes into training. If you've never run a marathon before, you might be shocked at how the preparation can quickly take over your life. Scheduling hours-long runs in the early morning or evening hours, attending weekend road races to qualify for the big event, realizing there are certain foods that can actually make it harder for you to run (and then overhauling your diet accordingly)—and now, this time, managing all that with two kids. It was going to be tough. But I was determined to do it.

When I was in college at St. Lawrence University, I signed up for a writing class on a whim. I had never written more than an essay, and I didn't know where to begin the process of writing a story. One of the assigned books was *Bird by Bird: Some Instructions on Writing and Life* by Anne Lamott. In the book, Lamott recalls a scenario that played out at the kitchen table in her childhood home.

> Thirty years ago, my older brother, who was ten years old at the time, was trying to get a report on birds written that he'd had three months to write. It was due the next day. We were out at our family cabin in Bolinas, and he was at the kitchen table close to tears, surrounded by binder paper and pencils and unopened books on birds, immobilized by the hugeness of the task ahead. Then my father sat down beside him, put his arm around my brother's shoulder, and said. "Bird by bird buddy. Just take it bird by bird."

That passage has stuck with me since the day I read it in that first class. I've said the phrase "bird by bird" so many times in my head when I felt overwhelmed by a task. That is how I would approach the marathon, and more importantly the enormous task of training for it. Bird by bird. Mile by mile.

So as the first step toward my 26.2 mile marathon, I signed up for a four-miler training race, the first one I'd attempted since I crossed my last marathon finish line in almost ten years.

I stressed about those four miles for days before the race. I hadn't run more than a mile or maybe two in the years between the marathon and now. I talked with Ryan incessantly in the days leading up to this race about whether or not I'd be able to finish without walking.

Ryan is not a patient person, and grows easily frustrated with conversations that have no real purpose or possible resolution within the conversation's timeframe. In other words, there was no way for him or me to know how I would feel during the race so why were we discussing it?

One of the downfalls of being a type-A person (me) married to another type-A person (or, as my mother refers to the two of us "Double A and Triple A") is that we are both masters of efficiency. As such, there is no tolerance for speculation or rambling conversation. Things needed to Get. Done. Now.

He'd be bringing Addie and Will to the race, and I'd signed Addie up for the three-year old sprint race after the adult race was over—her first New York Road Runners event.

I fretted more about the race, I think, than I would have had she not been going to attend with Ryan and Will. I wanted so much to model good behavior for her, for her to see me finish strong. I mentioned this to an exasperated Ryan and said that I was worried I'd have to stop, I'd have to give up midrace.

He didn't even look up from the dishes he was loading into the dishwasher. "Well," he said, "you've never given up on anything in your life. I really doubt you're going to start with this."

It's funny, the things we worry we can't do when, if we just look back on our lives, we've already faced things that were so much harder and come out on the other end perfectly intact and often better than we were before. I had, in the last two years, come through what was undoubtedly the scariest and most painful thing I had ever faced in my life: Will's prenatal Down syndrome diagnosis. There were nights, moments, when I literally thought I was going to die from the pain. All I saw was darkness. Shadows and fears and monsters at every turn.

I realized Ryan's words were entirely correct. There wasn't actually any doubt in my mind that I'd be able to finish a simple four-mile loop around Central Park. I stopped talking.

And so, on an early spring day, I pinned my number to my shirt, tied on my shoes, ate a banana, and ran the race. It was a breeze, actually, and I couldn't believe I'd let it stress me out as it had. And there at the finish line was my team: Ryan, Addie, and Will, waiting and cheering.

A few minutes after I finished my race it was time for Addie's. So we pinned on her number and sent her on her sprint. It was about a quarter-mile.

Bird by bird.

Modeling Good Behavior: Why We Really Do All This

It occurs to me that this is the heart of this entire project, the transformation into the Happiest Mommy I can be. I'm trying to take small steps, slight changes in behavior and attitude, that will result in big—and lasting—change. Not just for us moms, but also for the children we love so much. If you were to ask yourself if you want your son or daughter to exercise regularly as an adult, I'm going to go out on a limb and say the vast majority of the population is going to answer a resounding yes. But without proper modeling, how is a child to know that a regular fitness routine is a desirable and entirely attainable part of a healthy and balanced life? This resolution is selfish, sure, but it's also (like all the resolutions in this project) made with a truly selfless end in mind: improving myself so I can model great behavior for my children.

And study after study shows that people who exercise have less stress, sleep better, and are overall healthier than those who don't.

When it comes to kids, the research that shows the benefit of regular exercise is vast: According to the Centers for Disease Control and Prevention, "Regular physical activity in childhood and adolescence improves strength and endurance, helps build healthy bones and muscles, helps control weight, reduces anxiety and stress, increases self-esteem, and may improve blood pressure and cholesterol levels."

The U.S. Department of Health and Human Services recommends that young people aged six to seventeen years participate in at least sixty minutes of physical activity daily, but only about one-quarter of adolescents did so, according to a 2013 report from the same organization.

The benefits of exercise in kids are one thing—certainly reduced anxiety and stress and increased self-esteem are both positive—but it's really the CDC's warnings of the possible consequences of inactivity that scared the pants off me:

- "Overweight and obesity, which are influenced by physical inactivity and poor diet, can increase one's risk for diabetes, high blood pressure, high cholesterol, asthma, arthritis, and poor health status."
- "Physical inactivity increases one's risk for dying prematurely, dying of heart disease, and developing diabetes, colon cancer, and high blood pressure."

Dying prematurely.

It occurs to me as I read this on the CDC's website that the primary goal of parenting, as I understand it, is to keep your children alive. Like that's the number-one basic thing we're all trying to do, right? But there're a million ways, it seems, to kill someone before their time, and once we've locked up the cleaning products, hovered at bath time, and purchased the top-of-the line car seat and had it professionally installed, there's still much to be done.

Immediately my thoughts turn to what other activities I can get the kids involved with. They need to learn to love exercise! Or else, I think to myself, they are destined to a life of chip eating on the couch and morbid obesity that leads to that premature death I just read about.

But hold on one minute. If a parent is a child's greatest teacher, something I wholeheartedly believe to be true, then it might be enough, at least for now, to focus on my own exercise and overall physical health and to simply let them see.

You know how, growing up, there were weird things your parents and family did that you had no idea were weird until you were an adult?

When I was growing up, there was an index card taped to the wall in our bathroom, next to our toilet. It was carefully hand-lettered by Dad, in big block letters instructing us to use only four squares of toilet paper. "4 Squares, 4 Times, then flush. Repeat if necessary" it read. I didn't question it. Those were the rules.

When I went to visit my friends' houses, I was surprised to see that there were no rules governing toilet paper square use in their households; I guess I just assumed something had happened to the signs in their bathrooms. That they'd run out of tape or whatever. I literally had no clue until college that this particular obsession with the toilet paper was specific to the Shaw family. But by then it was too late. I was already in the habit. Maybe if I had given it any real thought, I would have realized the oddity of the toilet paper sign, but I didn't because it was simply part of my life.

When potty training Addie, I explained to her that for the purposes of efficient wiping, plus toilet paper conservation, plus low-toilet clogging risk, the optimal number of squares to use is almost always four.

Obviously.

Ryan's family has a thing about soda. Whenever they would go out to dinner when Ryan and his sister were children, they would order only one drink for the whole family. Ryan's parents still share one drink when we go out to dinner with them. I have no idea why. And guess who never, ever orders his own drink when we find ourselves at a fast-food restaurant on a road trip? You got it. Ryan.

What if, instead of toilet paper, the Shaw family "quirk" had centered around physical activity? I know for a fact that my dad didn't make the toilet paper sign with the hopes that someday my brothers and I would pass along this gem to our own children, but that's exactly what happened. My nieces and nephew are equally as diligent in their usage.

If family physical activity was as much a part of Addie and Will's life as those toilet paper guidelines were a part of mine, I think I'd stand a pretty good chance of passing along some positive habits and attitudes when it comes to working out.

So with that in mind, the marathon training continued, and I was far more—though not totally—guilt free, knowing that in doing something for myself, something that made me feel great, I was modeling to them what would be their "normal."

The normal I was looking to model, however, went beyond incorporating exercise into our family life. It's been shown in numerous studies that exercise reduces stress, something I desperately needed to do.

To say I manage stress poorly is an understatement. I'm what people refer to as a yeller. My stress manifests itself in the form of lashing out. It gets exponentially worse if I'm overtired. I'm also an anxious person, but have never and have no interest in taking medication to control my anxiety. It's not social anxiety or anything like that—it's more the frequent feeling of being at the beginning stages of a panic attack. I think about what needs to be accomplished in any given day, then how there are not possibly enough hours in that day to do all of those things, and then how I haven't even factored into that list actually spending quality time with my kids, and then there's the guilt and then the stress and before I know it I'm yelling at someone about something that really isn't important at all.

It would seem the last thing to do would be to add something else—like exercise—to the plate. But if exercise helps reduce stress, therefore making the time spent with your family better, therefore making you a happier mom, and therefore having happier children—isn't it worth it?

According to the Anxiety and Depression Association of America (ADAA), seven out of ten adults in the United States say they experience stress or anxiety daily, and most say it interferes at least moderately with their lives. And while the people surveyed have different ways of coping—ranging from exercise to speaking with friends to eating to watching TV to sleeping—the association touts exercise as the one most recommended by medical professionals.

"The physical benefits of exercise—improving physical condition and fighting disease—have long been established, and physicians always encourage staying physically active. Exercise is also considered vital for maintaining mental fitness, and it can reduce stress. Studies show that it is very effective at reducing fatigue, improving alertness and concentration, and at enhancing overall cognitive function. This can be especially helpful when stress has depleted your energy or ability to concentrate.

"When stress affects the brain, with its many nerve connections, the rest of the body feels the impact as well. So it stands to reason that if your body feels better, so does your mind. Exercise and other physical activity produce endorphins—chemicals in the brain that act as natural pain-killers—and also improve the ability to sleep, which in turn reduces stress.

"Scientists have found that regular participation in aerobic exercise has been shown to decrease overall levels of tension, elevate and stabilize mood, improve sleep, and improve self-esteem. Even five minutes of aerobic exercise can stimulate anti-anxiety effects."

I knew that I wouldn't be able to get out for a run every morning—it's just not fair to put the morning routine on your spouse every day, and I couldn't sustain for several days in a row waking up at five in order to get back in time to shower before the kids rose. Still, I knew that the days I got in some form of physical activity were better days than the ones I didn't.

I remembered that in addition to the Exhale on the Upper East Side where I live there's another studio on Central Park South, about a ten-minute walk from my office. The class is sixty minutes long. Core Fusion, while challenging, isn't a sweat-inducing workout, though, so I could definitely skip the postclass shower. I calculated I could be away from my desk for a total of ninety minutes midday and hit up a class.

So I brought a set of workout clothes to the office and kept them in a drawer. I thought about my average day and realized there was a definite pattern: a flurry of activity and emails in the morning straight through until about 11 a.m., when stories are being pitched, assignments are being made, and coverage is decided. Then begins the outreach to sources and experts, the photo and video requests for supporting assets. But around 11:30, things start to settle down for a few hours as you wait for return calls and emails, for photos and videos to be processed.

I started using that time for Core Fusion classes. To be sure, if there was something at work that conflicted—like an interview or a shoot, Core Fusion didn't happen that day. But if I knew in advance that was going to happen, I tried to make that morning a run morning to free myself up for the remainder of the day. With the workouts I was able to schedule during the week, plus one morning a weekend, I was getting in some form of activity four or five times each week. Nothing at work suffered, nothing at home suffered. I missed out on about an hour of time on the Internet each day, but I think that we'd all be better off with a little less Facebook, anyway.

Bird by bird and mile by mile, the running increased. The stress lessened. The weight started falling off. The Runkeeper app on my phone became one of my life's greatest pleasures: with every five minutes of running that passed, the robotic female voice came up as the music I was listening to lowered in order to alert me to my progress.

"Time. Thirty. Five. Minutes. Distance. Three. Point. Six. Miles. Average Pace. Nine. Minutes. Fifty-Two Seconds. Per Mile."

The app keeps a record of your runs, so it was easy to track my progress. In May, I was averaging about five miles per run. June, I was up to six. I peaked in July when I hit eight miles on an average run, and was doing it a few times per week. I felt great. I felt happy. The experiment was working.

However, I knew those eight miles in July would likely be the longest I would run for a while. And it was around that same time I had to let LuMind know I wouldn't be able to run the marathon this year after all. Because it was a couple months prior to that when I found out I was pregnant with our third child.

Ryan and I had talked about a third child. Not with any formality really, but more along the lines of a sentimental chat as we watched Addie and Will grow up so fast and we both said we would be "open" to the idea of a third baby. So it was with that open-mindedness that our baby was conceived shortly thereafter.

Our journey to parenthood was not an easy one. Addie is the result of several years of trying. Medical intervention was not successful. But then one day, after we decided to "take a break," I was pregnant.

With Will, no medical intervention was needed to conceive, though it didn't happen immediately. It was soon after I found out that I was pregnant, however, that major medical intervention began. He was diagnosed at just twelve weeks gestation and we were warned of, and monitored for, many health conditions, including a heart problem, none of which he ended up having.

During that time it was all I could do to get up each day. Working out wasn't really on the table. I decided this time could be different. For a while, I even had it in the back of my mind that I would still run the marathon. I would be seven months pregnant, I calculated. Didn't some woman run the marathon eight months pregnant recently?

Indeed. Amy Keil ran the Boston Marathon in April of

2015 when she was thirty-four weeks pregnant. I brought this up to my doctor when I tentatively asked him what he thought about my running the marathon, too.

"It's not that you can't," he said. "But I think you really need to ask yourself if you believe you should."

I knew the answer. But I couldn't accept it still. So I casually brought the matter up in conversation with my father, knowing he would have the words of wisdom. My father, when I was a child, was a teller. By that I mean I was told what to do, when and how to do it, with very little tolerance for discussion. As an adult, things could not be more different. He never, ever tells me what to do—even when I'm practically begging him to.

And with regards to the marathon, he simply said, "I don't think this situation is a matter of weighing the chances of something going wrong, which are quite small. It's about the consequences if they in fact do."

Which could be quite serious.

And with that the decision about the 2015 marathon was made. I was assured by the organization I had a number waiting for me next November and they'd be happy to have me back on the team.

But the training I had done so far wasn't for naught. It so happened that as I was really getting back into my running, I was also entering a critical time in my early pregnancy. The baby was undergoing the same prenatal tests that had led to Will's diagnosis. First a screening, followed by chorionic villus sampling (also known as CVS), then a more extensive screening called a DNA microarray. The CVS would tell us with certainty about trisomy 21 (Down syndrome) and about trisomies 18 and 13. The chromosomal microarray, also called a CMA, looks in detail at every single chromosome to check for microdeletions, among other things, that can cause issues ranging from very mild to very significant in a person's life.

It is absolutely terrifying.

Of course we discussed not doing any testing at all. And there's a certain kind of person, a kind that I have great respect for, who can choose that path. I am not that person. I knew I had to know, as much as I could, what the future might look like for our child.

Now I must step up on my hypothetical soapbox for a moment. There is no test, genetic or otherwise, that can tell you anything about your child's smile, laugh, love, and ability to better the life of everyone in his life. This is clearly the case with Will. He is everything I always wanted and nothing any doctor said he would be. I shudder to think of my life without him in it, because we are infinitely happier since his birth.

Similarly, there's no test that will tell you if your kid will be walking across the street one day and be hit by a cab and spend the rest of his or her life needing your assistance. Or if she will fall in with the wrong crowd and become a drug addict, or end up in an abusive relationship.

So I realize the limits of these tests, of course. I also know (now) firsthand that what they tell you about your child and who they will be is being communicated through a very narrow lens, and though you'll know for sure that the 47th chromosome will bring challenges, it tells you absolutely nothing about the other 46. The ones that make up 97.87234042553192 percent of who your baby is.

It didn't change the fact that I was scared.

My eyes had been opened. I knew, since entering the world of special needs, that Down syndrome was in many ways a cakewalk. Down syndrome has support groups and Buddy walks and research centers and a proven track record of advocacy. It has famous people! Parents of children with Down syndrome long before us had blazed the trail of inclusion, built schools, fought for legislation, and generally made our lives much, much easier.

It wasn't like that for everyone. Some people lose their children. There could be no worse pain than that.

So I humbly step off my soapbox now, and return to the weeks in which baby number three was undergoing these tests. The day I was to receive the call regarding whether or not the baby had one of the trisomies happened to be the same day I was meeting with publishing houses to see if anyone wanted to buy this book and the same day I was shooting a segment for *Good Morning America* in Connecticut on saving money on groceries. Talk about stress. As I chatted up the book and listened to the various questions asked of me, it was as if I was watching myself from somewhere else. It was like being underwater, where you know other people are there but they are all blurry and the voices are muffled.

Once I wrapped up the meetings and got in the car to go to Connecticut, I was on the verge of a complete and total meltdown. No call. The battery on my phone was dying and I arrived at the shoot to find out the family we were shooting with and the producer were running about an hour behind schedule. So I had the driver take me to a Dunkin' Donuts, where I plugged in my phone and stared at it. I knew I should have been reviewing the notes for the shoot but I couldn't. No call.

We got to the grocery store where I met the perfectly lovely couple whom I would be assisting in cutting back on their astronomically high grocery bill. My mic pack went on and I asked the sound technician how I would turn it off if I needed to take a call. It wouldn't work, given that it was under my dress, so I made him promise to turn off the sound on his equipment if I got on the phone. I couldn't hold my phone and also walk the couple around the store during the segment, so I had Natasha, the producer (who must have thought I was insane), hold the phone as she followed behind the cameraman.

I walked with the couple through the store—a Stop & Shop in Guilford, Connecticut—comparing the costs of coffee and explaining to them that the best bargains were often found at the end of the aisles. *ARE WE REALLY TALKING ABOUT THIS?* the voices were screaming inside my head. *WHY DO YOU EVEN CARE ABOUT ORGANIC BLUEBERRIES? CAN'T YOU SEE THAT IF THAT PHONE RINGS, I AM GOING TO THROW UP ALL OVER YOU AND THIS GROCERY STORE FLOOR?*

But I smiled and chatted and offered my very best advice. And I saved them over $4k annually in groceries. A lovely woman from the bakery department made me a cake in the shape of a minion that said "Good Minion America!"

The whole thing felt like an out-of-body experience.

Still, no call.

It was about 4 p.m. when I finally called the doctor myself. I was told he would call me back before the close of business.

At 5 p.m. there still was no call. I called back. The office was closed.

That night was a sleepless one. When I got home from the shoot, Ryan told me that he had also called the office and asked for the test results. He was told that the paperwork had been received from the hospital, but they couldn't share the results with him, only me.

Which of course left us reeling. Why would the doctor not call us?

As the sun came up the next morning, I hadn't slept more than an hour or two. I was conflicted. On the one hand, of course I didn't want my child to face any unnecessary challenges in life. But on the other hand, Will was such an incredible, amazing little boy and I wouldn't change one chromosome in his little body. Yes, not even the 47th.

At 5 a.m., when it was clear no more sleep would be coming, I decided to put on my running shoes and head to Central Park. Eighty minutes of running, soul searching, music pounding, and struggling to breathe later, I walked back to the apartment and got in the shower.

I felt better than I had in days. My body was exhausted but my mind was clear. I knew deep down that whatever the test results said, everything would be OK. Because I had Ryan. Because I had Addie. Because I had Will. And because I had this baby, who I knew I would love as intensely as I did the others.

And then, at 7:59, the phone rang. I knew the number. I just said, "Hi."

The woman's voice on the other end, the receptionist at the office, said that the initial round of testing from the CVS came back with no trisomies.

You might think I was relieved. Certainly a part of me was. But there was sadness, too. I don't expect anyone who hasn't been in this exact situation to understand this. Sadness that this child would in some ways *not* be like his or her older brother, who is total and complete perfection.

The run had cleared my head and given me the clarity I was looking for better than any $200-an-hour shrink session could have. As I waited for the results of the microarray in the coming days, I ran regularly. And by the time the day actually came for that call, I was surprised when the doctor's number once again popped up on my screen.

It was all fine. Whatever, I guess, *fine* means. By that time, I had let so much go. I had the answers I was looking for. I just needed the time to clear my head of all the clutter, the time to be alone with my thoughts, the time to reflect on how strong I already was, we were, and how there was nothing in this world—certainly nothing from a test result—that would get in the way of my, of our, happy life. Not one thing a person on the other end of the phone could tell me that would change the love I had for our unborn baby.

I needed the time to run. And thankfully, I found it.

Chapter 8

Hit the Family Lotto

Give Thanks for the One You Have

So, it had been several months since I first started this project in an effort to get happier. I thought it was time to check in with myself. Was it working?

Well, when it came to my diet, I was definitely doing (and feeling) a lot better, most of the time. And even though I was trying to "put myself first" in this experiment, now that I was "eating for two," I had even more cause to be thoughtful, deliberate, and careful with my food. It felt good.

I was keeping to my resolution of carving out some quality time with my friends once in a while, too. I didn't totally ditch the playdates for my kids (come on, I'm not a monster!), but I did scale them back a bit, and I was getting better at scheduling regular times to get together with *my* nearest and dearest, too. And once I had decided to open myself up to the mom friends I had met, I was even happier.

I was also feeling a lot more rested, thanks to the makeover I gave my bedtime routine. It had been hard to break our nighttime TV/iPad habit, but after several months my husband and I really were going to bed at a set time (mostly) and sleeping more soundly, waking more rested. Now that I was pregnant, I craved (nay, demanded) sleep every night. The positive results on the rest of my day were tangible.

Now that my tummy was expanding, my wardrobe issues took on a new, ahem, dimension. I did invest in a few snazzy maternity outfits for the office. I also gave myself the occasional pass on wearing black workout pants at other times. They were sooo comfy. And besides, what else was going to fit my ever-growing girth?

My husband and I were being more patient with each other, and now that I was back on a set schedule of ob-gyn appointments (along with those chiropractor sessions for my back) I was definitely seeing the doctor regularly again. While my marathon training was on hold, I was still active and feeling good about moving my body again. Overall, I felt more in control of my life and my destiny. Less frazzled. More, dare I say, *happy*?

One of the big reasons for my happiness, however, is something I can take no credit for whatsoever. Call it fate, call it luck, I don't know. It's this: before I even became a mommy myself, I hit the lottery when it came to my family. And that has certainly made me very happy indeed, both before I started this little experiment, and certainly as it progressed.

Two loving parents and two wonderful older brothers. Those brothers married lovely women who I am proud to call my sisters-in-law. And between them, they have four wonderful, loving kids whom I simply adore.

I did nothing to deserve them all. And it occurs to me that

people who have crappy parents or siblings may have also done nothing to deserve having to put up with *those* people in their lives. I imagine that having crappy parents or awful siblings probably makes life a lot harder, because I know that even when those relationships are bad, they are major ones in life and they can take up a lot of emotional room.

When I look at my kids and see how much they love each other, I hope that never changes, and I pray that I'm modeling the same kind of loving family relationships to them that I've always felt in my own life. I'm pretty good. I tell my mom and dad all the time how much I appreciate and respect them. I love my brothers deeply. But I could be better. I vow to try: I'm going to work hard to show my mom, my dad, and my two brothers how much I care for them.

Respect Thy Mother

My mother takes care of our kids twice each week. And while they would never admit it, I think the reason my parents keep their apartment in the city is so that they can help us out with the kids. This means I have total peace of mind when my mother is with the children, knowing that if anyone in the world loves them as much as Ryan and I do, it's her. And in fact, she's better with them in many ways than I am.

She's the one who introduced me to tissues with lotion in them. I didn't realize wiping Will's nose with toilet paper and paper towels was irritating his skin so badly.

She forever worries about their comfort. Are they warm

enough? Too warm? Are those shoes too tight? Do they have the proper winter attire, including layers of fleece and down, boots and snowsuits and hats and mittens that won't get taken off?

And their laundry. Well, apparently I don't do it right. But she has devoted a shelf in one of my closets to a variety of different laundering materials and ironing accoutrements so their clothes are always kept in the best possible condition.

It's she who has remembered their "month birthdays" since their births, and shows up on that day of each month with gifts in hand. Are you confused about what a month birthday is? Me too, because I can assure you my "month birthday" wasn't celebrated when I was growing up. A month birthday is a gift-giving day on the same day of each month corresponding to the day of the month the child was born. Example: Addie was born on the third of October. On the third of *every* month, she gets gifts. Same goes for Will. But since he was born on the thirty-first, sometimes his gifts come on the thirtieth or the first.

I don't even remember their month birthdays.

She has come with us to Boston for ear tube surgeries and stayed up all night with them when they were sick and I was too tired to do it myself. She's met me at the pediatrician. She's been the mystery reader in Addie's pre-K class.

She has car seats in her car and high chairs and cribs in her house. She has held the children for hours and hours while they were sick or fussy.

Call me lucky. I am.

My dad, though less hands on, is equally as enamored

with his grandchildren—my kids and my brothers' alike. He makes sure he and my mother have DVRed the shows the kids like when they come to my parents' house. He proudly shares with me the successes of my brothers' kids and recounts with great joy the clever things Addie or Will did while they were under his and my mother's care. He attends plays and soccer games and concerts and grandparents' day, despite the fact that at more than seventy years old, he still works.

As it turns out, all that caring has likely shaped me into an overall happy adult. A long-term study, done at University College London (UCL), found that those who perceived their parents as more caring and less psychologically controlling were likely to be happier and more satisfied throughout their lives. The study monitored the mental well-being of participants in the Medical Research Council (MRC) National Survey of Health and Development between the ages of 13 and 64. The survey tracked 5,362 people since their birth in 1946, of whom 2,800 remain under active follow-up: 3,699 participants had complete well-being data at ages 13 to 15, falling to approximately 2,000 by ages 60 to 64. Lead author, Dr. Mai Stafford from the MRC Unit for Lifelong Health and Ageing at University College London, explains on the UCL website: "We found that people whose parents showed warmth and responsiveness had higher life satisfaction and better mental well-being throughout early, middle and late adulthood. By contrast, psychological control was significantly associated with lower life satisfaction and mental well-being. Examples of psychological control include not allowing children to make their own decisions, invading their privacy and fostering dependence."

"We know from other studies that if a child shares a secure emotional attachment with their parents, they are better able to form secure attachments in adult life," said Stafford in the study. "Parents also give us a stable base from which to explore the world, while warmth and responsiveness has been shown to promote social and emotional development. By contrast, psychological control can limit a child's independence and leave them less able to regulate their own behavior."

My parents are that rare combination of incredibly supportive and yet not at all intrusive. They put virtually no demands on us whatsoever and also are there at the drop of a hat when needed. As a result, Ryan and I do our very best to do whatever it is we think will make them happy—going to a family party we'd like to otherwise skip or attending the funeral of a friend of theirs.

As it turns out, the impact of extended family on children may even be helpful to their educational success. Which, at least in my family, seems quite true: my mother, a former math teacher, has spent quite a bit of time teaching Addie addition and subtraction, patterns and more—things they haven't gotten to in her preschool yet.

The 2013 study done by Mads Meier Jaeger, a professor at the University of Copenhagen, found that the extended family's role in educational success was of particular importance among lower-income families and mattered less in higher-income families.

The positive emotional ramifications of extended family on a child seem indisputable. In a 2008 national survey carried out in the United Kingdom by Oxford University of more than 1,500 kids, it was found that grandparents who are involved in the upbringing of their grandchildren can contribute to a child's well-being.

This research was done in collaboration with the Institute of Education, London, and surveyed via questionnaire 1,596 children, ages eleven to sixteen from across England and Wales, and researchers conducted in-depth interviews with forty children from a range of backgrounds.

The survey revealed that grandparents often have more time than working parents to support young people in activities and are well placed to talk to their grandchildren about any problems the young people may be experiencing. The results also found that grandparents were involved in helping to solve the young people's problems as well as in talking with them about plans for their future. And those with a high level of grandparental involvement had fewer emotional and behavioral problems.

Judging from my many conversations with mom friends about the role of their own parents in their kids' lives, it would seem that grandparent-child-grandchild relationships are not always easy. Common issues that arise are too much or a lack of discipline from the grandparent over the child; grandparents who don't follow the rules the parent has set forth in regard to anything from food to bedtime to toys; grandparents who offer unsolicited advice to their children about child-rearing.

These issues are very common even among moms who have solid and loving relationships with their parents.

It may have to do with feeling judged. One of the curses of

motherhood is that, even when you're doing it well, it always feels like you're doing it wrong—or, at least, if you're doing it well in any given moment, it feels more than likely to be a fluke and all about to fall apart at any moment.

It's this way when it comes to my children's laundry. I feel quite ridiculous even bringing this up, because, as I've mentioned, I'm acutely aware of the actual challenges people face regularly when it comes to their family members. But it's a disagreement about laundry that seems to come up time and time again with my mother.

The short version, from my point of view: she's obsessed with laundry and ironing. This is not new to my children. When I was growing up, I wore a uniform to school. When I awoke each morning, my skirt and blouse were crisply ironed and hanging on my door.

I have not inherited this gene. I separate lights and darks. That's about it. I don't know where my ironing board is. My mom actually brought her own ironing board to our house. As I mentioned earlier, she has an entire shelf in one of our closets dedicated to laundry products, stain removers, fabric softeners, and wrinkle releasers.

From my mother's point of view, I don't take care of the children's clothes in the way they should be taken care of, especially considering how much I paid for them. And she says she doesn't mind at all taking care of the kids' clothes for me, so why do I complain about it? She certainly isn't looking for any kind of praise; in fact, she barely mentions it.

At some point during this journey to being the Happiest Mommy, I realized that I just simply had to stop thinking that I wasn't doing enough when every piece of objective evidence stated otherwise. I had to accept that there are things important to other people that just aren't important to me. Case in point: laundry. I decided instead to try to be grateful that I had someone in my life who did care, and who was willing to take on the laundry for me. One less thing for me to do, right?

But when it would seem all research on the topic points to the fact that more involvement from grandparents is preferable to less—and, judging from the joy you see on a child's face when they're with those grandparents—it makes sense to keep those relationships strong if they're already intact or attempt to mend them if not.

In the region of Durham in Ontario, Canada, the department of healthy families offered these five tips for keeping the peace among extended family on its web site:

1. Communication: As with most conflict, communication is vital to resolving the situation. It is important to discuss differences sooner rather than later. Let parents know their help is appreciated, and although you may disagree, the decision regarding your child's well-being is yours to make.

2. Try to listen. Conflict can escalate when the people involved do not listen to each other, thus it is important to stay calm and actively listen to what your parents have to say.

3. Be precise. Set clear roles and boundaries with your parents. Setting boundaries does not mean grandparents cannot have authority, but it is important for them to understand their authority is under your discretion.

4. Stay composed. It is important to address the conflict and not the individual. Anger can cause us to lash out at the other person instead of addressing the actual issue. Let your parents know how you feel in addition to listening to how they feel.

5. Respect. Avoid any verbal or nonverbal actions such as eye rolling, which conveys disrespect for the other person. Although you do not agree when it comes to your parent's opinion, you should respect that they are individuals who are entitled to have feelings different than your own.

Honor Thy Brother

I'm not going to pretend there aren't things about my family that drive me crazy. There are. And I'm quite certain—so certain, in fact, that there's no need for me to ask them—that I do plenty of things to annoy them, too. But the ways they drive me nuts from time to time are really so incredibly minor in the grand scheme of the love that's there. So when those flare-ups happen, they also don't last too long.

My elder brother, Billy, and I had an epic fight on a family vacation last summer. It was my mother's birthday, and I had planned to have a party for her on the beach that evening. I took it upon myself to plan the event for the twenty-plus people we vacation with on Hilton Head Island annually. In my typical control-freak, er, *responsible* manner, I tackled this party down to the last detail. I purchased the food, the cake, the wine, and a few decorations. Made sure everyone knew where to meet and at what time.

Of course, the best-laid plans can still go awry. Just at the moment I was pulling up to the beach on my bike with a trailer filled with everything we would need to have a successful party, the skies parted. I had not until then, and have not since, seen rain like this. It came over the beach so fast and so furious, I was not worried about getting wet, I was worried for the safety of the kids. Addie was terrified, Will was screaming. Meanwhile, there were two giant beach tents that needed to be disassembled, not to mention walked to cars or back to the house, along with bags upon bags of food.

I was five months pregnant at the time and already a tad resentful that everyone else had been sitting on the beach for the last couple of hours while I pulled all the party items together. So when I looked over and saw Billy giving directions (but not actually doing anything to get everyone off the beach as far as I could tell), I lost it.

My brother is probably the kindest person I have ever met. He is the least judgmental of all of us. He is warm and loving. He also has a habit of not being what you might call proactive when it comes to doing things he might not enjoy—in this case, party planning.

I yelled at him to stop telling other people what to do and get off his ass and do it himself. There may have been some cursing; it's hard to remember. He was standing a few feet away, but it only took one second for him to react to my criticism; he came up to me, yelling in my face and finger pointing. It was pouring rain, we had an audience of twenty, and there we were, yelling at the top of our lungs about who was doing what.

I'll never forget one thing he said, though—he said something along the lines that I should stop being such a martyr all the time. He said that if I was going to be so pissed off at all the work I was doing, why was I doing it in the first place? No one told me to do it. No one asked me to do it. I took it upon myself to plan a party, and then was resentful when everyone else didn't fall in line the way I wanted them to.

You know what? He was right. It was a central theme in my life, actually. And I never forgot it.

Sometimes the people you love are the only ones who are going to shoot you straight. They hold a mirror up to you and force you to see yourself how you really are. It's not always pretty, and, thankfully, because they love you as much as they do, they bite their tongue far more often than not. But once in a while, they let you have it. And when someone you love dearly (and you know feels the same way about you) actually goes to that place that they know is going to hurt you, chances are it's something you needed to hear.

Like I did on that rainy night on the beach.

As is the norm when we rarely argue, it quickly passed. I apologized, he accepted, and apologized, too. And by the next day, we were fine again.

My brother Tim would probably never yell at me the same way Billy did. I'm sure I do plenty to irritate him, too, but it's just not his style. He's really more the type to ice you out until whatever the issue is passes. I can't think of the last time we argued.

But Tim's also the type that's there the second you need him. When things get real, he's the one who is ready to face it with you, head on. After I found out Will would be born with Down syndrome, it was Tim I called over and over to ask for advice. It was Tim who took the train into the city and came to my office to take me to lunch and just sat there and listened, listened, listened to me while I tried to sort things out without offering even a drop of unwanted advice. He was the one who sent me an email telling me I was the best and bravest person he knew.

I think about that time often. I am forever grateful for his love. You know what else I'm grateful for? That with each one of my kids, in the early months of their lives when I was completely exhausted, Tim has either taken them overnight in his home or, if we were on a family vacation, gotten up with them in the night so that Ryan and I could sleep. And he doesn't half-ass it, either. I'm talking about sleeping on the floor next to their cribs, heating middle-of-the-night bottles and feeding them in the dark, and taking them on early-morning walks so that their cries didn't wake us from our slumber.

See? I told you I hit the family lotto.

I am so grateful.

Needless to say, I love them both very much. But it occurs to me that despite the fact that I am so hopeful that Addie and Will will grow up to be exceptionally close, the kind of siblings that talk all the time and hang out often, I don't do much to foster that kind of relationship with my own brothers. The fact that we are able to count on one another seems more a stroke of luck than anything I'm actually doing to facilitate it.

In what's been called the greatest graduation speech ever, the subject of siblings is addressed. The speech is oft attributed as having been given at MIT in the 1990s by Kurt Vonnegut.

But the speech was never given by Vonnegut. In fact, it was never given at all. It was a column written by Mary Schmich for the *Chicago Tribune* as a speech she would like to give to a graduating class.

It would seem that the greatest graduation speech of all time was never heard by a graduating class. It's unfortunate. Because it's filled with wisdom, not the least of which is "wear sunscreen." But it also offers food for thought on our sibling relationships: "Get to know your parents. You never know when they'll be gone for good. Be nice to your siblings. They're your best link to your past, and the people most likely to stick with you in the future."

Stick with you in the future. If there is one thing I can say for sure about my brothers, it's that they have stuck with me. This is not to say we spend hours chatting on the phone—ever—or all our weekends hanging out with each other. Far from it. Though we do see each other a fair amount, there can easily be a month or two that passes when we don't and our relationship consists mostly of periodic text messages. Yet, when something good or bad happens, they are always on the short list. First Ryan, then my parents, then my brothers. That's just how it goes.

I wish we had more of the "just called to chat" kind of relationship, but that's never been my style. Even with my Happiest Mommy life makeover challenge, I have to be realistic: that's not going to happen with my brothers—not with anyone. I always feel like if there's something I need you to know, I'll tell you in person or if it cannot possibly wait, then in that case, and in that case only, I'll give you a call.

But watching Addie and Will, I marvel at their love and

devotion toward each other. I find myself hoping they'll never grow apart. Addie dotes on Will, and in turn, he absolutely adores her. He goes to bed first and we always say, OK, give Addie a kiss—and he makes a beeline for her. They embrace, my heart melts. Ryan and I look at each other, so touched night after night by a love so pure.

How can I model positive sibling relationships for them? Clearly I need to work on being a better sister myself.

The Ties That Bind

Research shows that the closest sibling relationships are between sisters and the least close between brothers. Brother-sister relationships fall somewhere in the middle.

I vacillate between wishing I had a sister and being so thankful I don't. On the one hand I do envy the close bond so many sister pairs I know seem to share. On the other hand, many of those—not all, but many—are filled with drama and fights well into adulthood, even if they are otherwise close.

On the same trip as the rainstorm fight with Billy, there was a particular afternoon we were all sitting on the beach. Five months pregnant and in no mood to jump the waves for the tenth time that day, I told Billy, Addie's godfather, he should take her in the water. Billy is more of a sit-on-the-beach-and-hold-court kind of uncle than a play-in-the-water-and-keep-you-from-drowning kind of uncle, but I figured since I was sitting right there watching, not too much could go wrong.

Tim, it should be noted, is the opposite. He's exactly the

keep-you-from-drowning kind of uncle. There are three people in the world I trust to take my kids in the water if I am not present. Tim, Ryan, and my mom. In that order.

But Billy agreed, and into the water they went. As they walked into the surf, backs to me, I yelled out jokingly, "Make memories!"

A few minutes later, they were headed out of the water toward the beach again. *That's it?* I thought. *Couldn't he keep her a little longer?*

But even from several yards away I could see that while Addie was skipping out to the sand and smiling, Billy was wincing in pain.

"What happened?" I asked. There was a stream of blood coming down his foot by his ankle.

"I don't know," he said, and described a sudden, sharp pain.

"You think it was a jellyfish?" I asked. The waters were known for them, though no one had suffered a sting so far that vacation.

"I don't think so," he said. "Maybe I just stepped on a sharp shell or something."

It didn't sound right. There weren't really any sharp shells in this water—the sand was actually remarkably soft. And there was no debris around whatsoever, so glass or something similar also seemed unlikely.

He's not much of a complainer, but for the rest of the day I could see he was in some pain. As the day turned to night, the pain wasn't going away. It was also spreading.

Sometime after the rest of us went to bed, and only Ryan and Billy remained awake, Ryan convinced Billy to go to the twenty-four-hour urgent care center on the island. They arrived there around midnight, and as Billy described it, although the blood was coming from his Achilles tendon area, the most significant pain was down by his toes.

Turns out he had stepped on a stingray, and its barb had gone six inches into his foot. It was still in there, waiting to be extracted by a somewhat horrified doctor.

He was prescribed antibiotics because apparently stingray barbs are not at all sanitary and the serrated edges—think steak knife blade—can leave behind bacteria as the barb is pulled out of your foot. Worse, they can even leave pieces of their barb behind, though from the X-ray, it didn't seem that had been the case for Billy.

Ryan and Billy got home in the wee hours of the morning, and as we all awoke and heard the story of the night spent in urgent care, I was surprised at Billy's next words: "I'm just so glad it happened to me and not to Addie or you."

Addie was just a step behind Billy as they played in the water. And I was pregnant, so who knew if I would have been able to take the antibiotics prescribed.

But his words touched me deeply. Now, of course, any caring adult would wish for his or her own pain above that of a child. It was more the fact that that thought was at the forefront of his mind even as he was still in a lingering degree of pain.

Make memories indeed.

I'm not sure what the "right" way to have an adult sibling relationship is. I'm sure that I've seen some that seem entirely too close for my comfort level. I've seen ones in which one sibling wants a lot more than what the other is willing or capable of giving. I've seen plenty that are absolutely, irrevocably broken.

I do know from my own experience that having people to count on in tough times—people whom you know are not going anywhere, no matter what—is a gift. I think it's one that I was just given, probably to a large degree by my own parents who drilled something into my head when I was young.

I can remember being young, fighting with my brothers. I would routinely tell my mother that I "hated" whichever one of them I felt had wronged me that particular day.

My mother would say in response—and I'm paraphrasing—"This family is all you have and the only thing that matters. There is no one more important in your life than your brothers. They will be with you longer than any friend and long after your father and I are gone."

It stuck with me. And it's a sentiment I try to pass along to Addie and Will, and one I hope to instill in baby number three. Though at this stage in their lives, Addie and Will have nothing but mutual adoration for each other.

Research supports what my mother was telling me: sibling relationships are among the deepest, most important and long lasting of our lives. It makes sense that we would be devoted to a person who shares half our genetic makeup. But that devotion, which seems to come so naturally to young children, is harder to maintain as the years go by.

According to the Harvard Study of Adult Development, a seventy-five-year-long study of three hundred men, 93 percent of the men who were thriving at sixty-five had been close to a sibling in their early life. The study also reports that poorer relationships with siblings before the age of twenty could be a predictor of depression later in life, suggesting that the longer we can sustain close sibling relationships in adulthood, the more it can benefit and protect us emotionally.

Turns out if we want our kids to have emotionally satisfying lives, especially in their older age when we are long gone, it's worthwhile to foster those sibling relationships as best we can through the years—and in order to do so, to model close relationships with our own siblings, if we're lucky enough to have them.

Chapter 9

Leave Your Kids at Home

Take a Vacation Without Them Once in a While

Before we had kids, my husband and I were intrepid travelers. A honeymoon in Bali. A ten-day jaunt to Thailand. Long-weekend ski trips to France, Italy, and Whistler, BC. The week-long road trip down the California coast. The trip to the heavenly, if incredibly faraway Mauritius, more than seven hundred miles from Madagascar. And trips to every state from Maine to Florida. I worked for several years at the travel website Travelocity. I had insider access to amazing deals on great vacations, and the best part? Traveling around the world was, in fact, part of the job description.

And I did my job very, very well.

But if you asked me—and Ryan—about our trips since Addie was born, you'd meet a much more modest version of our prechild selves.

Before Addie was born, we swore up and down we'd never turn into those parents that bemoaned travel with kids as too hard to do. We reassured ourselves with lively discussions about how much our kids would learn on their trips: how well traveled they would be, how worldly and cosmopolitan.

True to our word, Addie started her travels right away. There was the ski trip to Colorado when she was five months old, and the week spent in a villa in Tuscany when she was eight months old. We visited wineries with her strapped to one of our chests in the baby carrier; we dined out each night as she sat quietly, being doted on by the lovely Italians we met. We put her to bed each night and sat on our patio sipping wine, congratulating ourselves on not becoming "those parents."

Addie stayed compliant for a while, doing great on our annual family trips to the Outer Banks and Hilton Head the spring and summer after she was born.

And then Addie began to walk.

Suddenly our cooperative, agreeable daughter was having none of sitting still on an airplane for five, six, or seven hours. None of it. Flying, even for the two hours it took to get to Savannah or the three it took to get to Florida, was dreaded. Her last international trip was a disastrous flight to the Caribbean prior to Will's birth. After a four-hour flight, plus a ferry to our hotel, a screaming Addie in tow the entire way, I was ready to never fly with a baby ever again.

And about two years later, I've largely kept that vow! As a family, we've flown to Florida twice and Hilton Head annually. We do a lot of driving vacations now, and we just got back from our very first camping trip, Addie's request at the end of her first year of pre-K.

It was the camping trip that got me thinking, *This is something that I never, ever would have spent my precious free time doing just three short years ago.* But once I found out Addie wanted to go camping? Research, inquiries to various places, poring over the list of "amenities" for each site, about fifty emails exchanged with Ryan on the various pros and cons of each site.

And once we were there? Building fires, fishing, a fire truck ride: all things designed to make Addie and Will happy.

It brought me back to a trip we took a few months ago, to Disney World. My job usually requires a minimum of one trip to Orlando per year (my company, ABC, is owned by Disney), but I always went alone, until this trip.

Addie, Will, and Ryan joined me for a little work and several days of play. We spent days in the Magic Kingdom, Addie had a makeover at the Bibbidi Bobbidi Boutique, we visited princesses and ate theme park food. We took a boat cruise to get the best possible view of the fireworks. It was the best first trip to Disney I could ever imagine.

But when I got home, I finally understood when parents said they needed a vacation from their vacation.

It's not that I mind planning trips with the kids in mind—after all, we're all in this family together. But it occurs to me that something that was just a short time ago one of the main focuses of my life—my hobby, if you will—is all but gone. Which, when you think about it, seems profoundly unfair. Ryan and I spend countless hours either working, engaged in child care, or tending to the requirements of adult trappings of bills and therapists and doctors' appointments day in and day out. Who really needs the vacation here? Aren't my kids kind of on vacation every day of their young lives? It was time to follow my motto in all other aspects of my life and put myself first in this part of the parenting equation: I needed a vacation. No kids. Stat.

The Beauty of a Kid-Free Vacation

While many of my Happiest Mommy guidelines are pretty noncontroversial, this one was proving to be rather unpopular. An oft-cited study from the U.S. Department of Education apparently found that kids who travel more have higher academic achievement and will earn more money in life than their nontraveling counterparts. You can imagine how the travel industry—hotels, cruise lines, time-shares, everyone you can think of—uses this study to their advantage. Now I can't seem to find any actual record of the study, but it's been quoted enough that you can bet that whether or not the "journalists" who covered it are correct in their analysis of the data, it's being taken at face value by moms and dads everywhere who don't have the media savvy to be hesitant to accept what they see on some blog as truth.

For some reason, this study absolutely enrages me.

It's not that I can't see how it could be accurate. But after all, aren't parents who have the means for travel likely the same parents who also have the means for after-school tutors, as an example? And if you're not the kind of mom who really feels like schlepping the kids on a trip to Europe this summer and would really just rather take them to the town pool, now you have to feel bad about that, too?

Enough is enough, I thought to myself. In defiance of a study I can't actually prove exists, I decided my kids were just fine, thank you very much. And though I would not stop traveling with them altogether, it was in all of our best interests if Ryan and I instead took advantage of our very loving and generous parents and left the kids with them while we and we alone took a few days away now and then.

One of our first weekends away was to New Orleans. We landed at about 10 a.m. and headed to the hotel. Our room at the Hotel Monteleone wasn't quite ready. But there was a room, they said, available, except usually no one wanted it, because it was in the middle of the hotel and didn't have a window. That seemed weird. But we were anxious to start the day and had a nearly-impossible-to-get lunch reservation in this city famous for its food in a couple of hours, so we said we would take it.

Here's a bit of advice from a person who has traveled a whole lot in her life. If you are an exhausted parent and you have the opportunity to go away for a weekend and sleep in a windowless room, you need to jump on that opportunity, stat. "Windowless room available" should be listed as an amenity on every single hotel website that is lucky enough to have one of these magical rooms. If it costs extra, you should pay extra. If you don't travel much, you may want to consider making such a room in your home.

Because I had not, since having kids, and have not since, slept as well as I did that weekend in the windowless room in New Orleans.

Ten hours spent on Bourbon Street barhopping—something that generally would cause a giant disruption to my sleep what with all the aspirin popping and water drinking that would have needed to occur—did nothing to disrupt the sleep. And we woke up the next morning with no sense of what time it was (close to ten, unheard of for us, even on a childless vacation), totally refreshed and ready for a day of sightseeing in NoLA.

If you take nothing else from this book, remember this: The next time you are so desperate for a good night's sleep you're on the verge of collapse, two words: windowless room.

That trip went so well that we decided not long after to take a long weekend in Iceland. Sounds exotic, but it's actually only a four-hour flight from New York to Reykjavik, making it entirely possible to visit for a long weekend.

I got violently ill before the trip. So much so that we considered canceling, but it had been a Christmas present for Ryan and very inexpensive, so therefore nonrefundable. I didn't want to lose the money, and Ryan's parents were coming down to watch the kids, so off we went.

I spent the first day of our trip in bed, in and out of sleep. It felt weird to be in Iceland, holed up in a hotel room (this one did have windows, sigh), but by the next day, I was feeling better, and we explored the city and rented a car to head out of town.

The only thing was that each day, when we called to Facetime with the kids, they were always half-dressed. And the lights were superdim in our apartment. Also, it was unclear what they were being fed; there was a lot of talk of snacks. But they seemed really happy to be with their grandparents, who they adore, and by all accounts were fine.

But control freak that I am, I was a little unsettled. *Why aren't they wearing the clothes I picked out for them?* I wondered. *And what's with the lights being so low?* I began to stress about clothes and lights and too many snacks being consumed when Ryan gave me a gem that is my mantra on people watching my kids even now.

"If people are going to be nice enough to come and watch your kids for free while you go on vacation, you really can't ask for more than that they're alive when you come home."

So true, right? After all, these are people—in this case, Ryan's parents, in other cases, my parents or my brothers—who love the kids deeply. If you want a break from the kids, you have to let go a little. In other words, it's not at all fair to expect everyone else to follow your rules and specifications. We were going away, after all. If I wanted everything done exactly the way I would do it, then I should probably stay home.

Which, after getting a taste of my prechild life, alone again with Ryan for a weekend here and there, was not going to happen.

We went to L.A. over my birthday and met up with Liz, a dear friend from college we hadn't seen in years. We talked about the good old days over drinks for hours before she took us to her favorite taco stand and ordered us an Uber back to the hotel. We happened upon the bar where Bravo shoots the reality show *Vanderpump Rules* and toasted with the members of the cast that were working that night. I think the kids back in New York with my parents for two nights had more fun with them than they would have had barhopping in Beverly Hills.

Another weekend we drove to Cape Cod, where Ryan's parents live, and dropped the kids off while we headed to a resort just a few miles away. It was our anniversary, and we had gotten engaged on Cape Cod.

It rained the entire weekend. It was the best thing that could have happened. As the rain came down in sheets, we felt no pressure to go anywhere at all, especially considering we were so familiar with the area anyway. We ate most of our meals at the resort and watched movie after movie. When we picked up the kids on Sunday, we were reconnected, and relaxed.

Most of these trips were taken in lieu of an exchange of gifts: Iceland was a Christmas gift, L.A. was my birthday, Cape Cod was our anniversary. And while the trips are far shorter and much closer to home than some of the more exotic ones we took prior to our kids being born, they accomplish the same goal: changing the scenery, spending time alone, actually having grown-up conversation, and relaxing. Plus, we both love travel, so it's a chance to share the excitement of a trip together.

We decided for our next getaway, we would travel somewhere farther afield, maybe for a week this time. We could split up the babysitting between my parents and his, we thought. I wanted to go to Nicaragua; Ryan wanted to go to Fiji. I of course also wanted to go to Fiji but it's a lot farther away and a lot more expensive than the beach shack in Nicaragua I was envisioning. As we debated the relative pros and cons of these vacations, time slipped away and all of a sudden we were running out of time to take the trip before it would be too late in my pregnancy with baby number three to fly.

In 2012, a woman named Rebecca Eckler penned a blog post for *Mommyish* in which she detailed her decision to take a vacation with her fiancé and leave her ten-week-old baby at home with his grandmother and nanny. Eckler is also the author of several books, including *Knocked Up: Confessions of a Hip Mother-to-Be* and *Mommy Mob: Inside the Outrageous World of Mommy Blogging*, something she no doubt is an expert on after the story about her leaving her infant at home went viral.

What actually happened: she left her infant son to go on a vacation. What you might think happened given the morning-show fodder, blog posts, comments on those posts, and vilification that followed: she left her child on the side of a highway and told him to play in traffic.

Some people even said she shouldn't have had a baby. Now that seems a bit extreme. Who judges at what age it's OK to get away for a while without the kids?

From her post: "Is me going away and leaving him behind a little selfish at his age? Um, absolutely. I admit that fully. Am I lucky to have such wonderful help? Um, absolutely. Will I miss him? Um, absolutely. But will I enjoy my vacation? Um, absolutely."

Some people actually speculated that Eckler must not be a real person, just a character to stir up controversy on a parenting blog. Because surely no one would actually do this—leave their ten-week-old for a vacation—right?

I'm just going to say it. I wouldn't have with Addie. I might have with Will. I absolutely would with baby number three, if there's someone out there willing to watch all three kids. (Hello? Anyone?)

So what actually happened was that we ended up on a Disney Cruise over Halloween weekend. With the kids, of course. Flight to Orlando, drive to Port Canaveral, on the ship to the Bahamas for the long weekend. Disney Cruises are great, and I recommend them to families often. But it wasn't quite the sipping cocktails on the beach while the kids were somehow off amusing themselves for hours at a time that I had envisioned.

My own experiences with childless vacations make me certain this isn't a hobby I'm going to give up at any point, even if people somehow think it makes me a bad parent. Sorry, not sorry, as the saying goes. What I really wanted to know, however, was if our kids even care about the family vacations we take together. The planning, the expense, the—let's face it—stress: what was it all for? "It's for the kids," parents say. So are the family vacations actually making the *kids* happy?

Thankfully, it appears the answer—from kids themselves— is yes. A survey from Harris Interactive on behalf of Project: Time Off of more than a thousand kids ages eight to eighteen found that more than half said vacations bring their families closer together and half said some of their best memories are of things they did during a family vacation.

Which might explain why, months later, Addie is still talking about the "Disney cru." And why when she draws a picture of our family, we are often depicted on the beach in Hilton Head or the Outer Banks.

I had long assumed that vacations make people happier. They certainly make me happier. Unless they make me more exhausted than I was prior to leaving for said vacation, in which case they do not make me happy at all. Instead, they make me annoyed that I spent time, energy, and money on something that in the end wore me out.

Americans, in general, are not good at taking vacations, or at least, not good at using all their vacation days. A 2015 study from Expedia, one of the world's largest travel booking sites, surveyed more than nine thousand people across twenty-six countries. Of the Americans surveyed, 92 percent said they felt happier after a vacation. So why are Americans leaving almost one-third of their vacation days on the table each year?

That was the finding of the study—that Americans have an average of fifteen days of vacation to use, but actually take eleven.

Part of the issue may be that when we're on vacation, we don't fully disconnect anyway. Can't blame our kids for that one. That's on us. There was a time, back in the early days of my globetrotting, that I actually didn't know how to operate my phone in a foreign country, and so I would just leave it behind. But now I know better, and my trips are more domestic than international anyway, so there it is in hand. I'm not alone—25 percent of workers worldwide claim to check their work email and phone messages once per day while on vacation.

I've been known to sneak in a little work on vacation myself. On that Disney cruise, in order to take full advantage of my whereabouts, I shot a video with Disney about the refurbished ship we were sailing on, which I then had produced for a story on the ABC News website. It seemed like the right thing to do—even though I had taken the time off work and was technically on "vacation."

"We continue to find that Europe's attitudes towards vacation are overall much different than North American and Asian attitudes," said John Morrey, vice president and general manager of Expedia.com, in a press release. "For some workers, vacation is a right, and for others, it's a guilty pleasure. Some workers also fear that their bosses will disapprove. A healthy work-life balance is critical, not only to give workers a chance to enjoy their lives outside of the office, but also to recharge, making you more productive when you get back to work."

That was partially what was behind the video. If I came back showing that I did some actual work on my trip, I felt less guilty about taking the days off in the first place.

Keep in mind that my vacation days, like most other people's, are a part of the compensation I agreed to when I took my job. So in essence, not taking those days is a lot like not being paid your agreed-upon salary. But it's not your employer's fault—at least not the majority of the time. It's yours. And if you choose to work when you're on vacation, you're again not being paid your agreed-upon salary.

I'm not going to pretend that I'm not lucky. You might think that in network news, taking vacation days is frowned upon. And if I was a political reporter taking time off the week before an election, yes, I could see how that would be a problem. But I'm not. I'm a lifestyle reporter who covers, among other topics, travel. And I have not ever been given one ounce of grief about a vacation, sick, or personal day in the entirety of my employment.

And yet. Emailing my coworkers and boss to show that I'm still connected. Shooting videos, conducting interviews, and taking story notes. Is it that I think I'm more important than I am? Or is it an insecurity that I am in fact not important enough?

You know who doesn't get paid vacation days? My kids. In fact, since we pay a pretty penny for them to go to school, I am losing money every time I take them out to go on a family trip. This has never once stopped me from pulling them out of school for a vacation, despite the fact that it is viewed as an unexcused absence. I imagine that as the kids get older, there may be actual consequences for them missing school, consequences that don't exist in the working world for taking the very days you're entitled to.

Not to mention that kids—likely because of their limited capacity to understand that what their parents are doing by taking them out of school for an unexcused absence is not exactly within the school rules—have no problem leaving the responsibility of school behind when they're traveling with their families.

It occurs to me that we could learn a lot from watching our kids on vacation. Wide-eyed wonder, ice cream galore, hours upon hours of fun with no cares outside of what's happening at that very moment.

Leaving what's at home—for us, the work and the stress; for them, school—where it belongs. At home. We ask them over and over, "Are you having fun?" But how often do we ask ourselves, "Are you having fun?"

Which, upon further reflection, seems at least as important as whether the kids are having fun or not. That said, it seems every parent I know plans their vacation with their children in mind first. What kind of activities will the resort have for children? Will there be food my kids will enjoy? Are there going to be other kids there for them to play with?

Of course, part of this is the same consideration you would extend to anyone in your life that you love. Right? If, say, you were going on vacation with an elderly grandparent, you might consider the accessibility of the pool. If your husband is a golf fanatic, as is mine, you might be inclined to choose a resort that has a golf course.

We take it to another level for our kids, though. Several parents I know travel with blackout shades so their kids' sleep won't be disrupted when the sun rises in their destination earlier than it rises at home.

What kind of consideration do mothers give themselves on family vacations? Not much, as far as I can tell. Mom's the one packing the beach bag, lathering everyone up with sunscreen, in the pool or playing lifeguard close by, planning every meal, executing every activity.

The first day of our last family beach vacation, I made a trip to the nearby Kroger to stock up on food for the kids and make sure the rest of the family at least had the essentials to get through the first day (we were the first of the group to arrive). While I was there, I saw a new(ish) book by an author I enjoyed—Nelson DeMille. When I was childless, reading DeMille books on the beach was something I did often. I'd head down with my chair and my book and sit for hours reading and intermittently chatting with whoever from the group showed up while I was there.

I decided I'd buy the book—after all, I was going to be in Hilton Head for two weeks. I could read that book in half a day if I had the time to myself. Surely two weeks would be enough time for it.

That night I read the first page and a half. And then I never picked it up again. At the end of the trip I told my mom to take it home with her.

"I'm never going to read it," I admitted.

Will, not yet two on this particular trip, decided he loved the water. The pool, the beach—didn't matter. The pool was far smaller of course, and it had a fence so at least he could be contained, so we started spending hours each afternoon there.

Two-year-old boys have little fear. Which means their mothers—in this case me—are in a constant state of panic about their safety. It did not occur to Will that he should have a fear of the water, so he didn't. So fast was he to plop himself in the pool that, prior to even going outside, I had to put on the swimmies that would keep him afloat.

So one day, desperate to avoid my daily poolside panic attack, my cousin Caitlin, who is one of the group of twenty on this annual vacation and who also happens to have attended the same college as Ryan and me so is a good friend, offered to accompany me on a two-hour drive to Charleston, where there was not only a great children's museum, she said, but a sandwich so good it was worth the drive.

When you're willing to spend four hours in a car with two kids under four instead of going to the beach or the pool, you've reached a new level of vacation stress. But that's what we did.

Kids on vacation are no less work than kids at home. In fact, when they are out of their element, off their sleep schedules, and existing on a diet of mostly ice cream and candy, there's an argument to be made that they are actually *more* work.

Never mind that parents and kids are often sharing a room, my absolute least favorite part of family vacations.

All of these factors might explain the whole "needing a vacation from your vacation" thing. But research shows that there might be happiness found in the simple planning of a vacation, rather than in the vacation itself. The aim of this study—published in the journal *Applied Research in Quality of Life*—was to obtain a greater insight into the association between vacations and happiness. It examined whether vacationers differ in happiness, compared to those not going on holiday, and if a holiday trip boosts posttrip happiness. These questions were addressed in a pretest/posttest design study among 1,530 Dutch individuals. 974 vacationers answered questions about their happiness before and after a holiday trip. Vacationers reported a higher degree of pretrip happiness, compared to nonvacationers, possibly because they are anticipating their holiday. Only a very relaxed holiday trip boosts vacationers' happiness further after return. In other words, thinking about and planning a trip had more of an effect on happiness than the trip itself.

Having now taken several vacations with the kids and stolen a few weekends away without, I have something to admit. And maybe it makes me a bad mother. But it's the truth. I am never going to be able to truly experience relaxation on a vacation unless I am taking that vacation without the kids.

There. I said it.

Don't get me wrong. The trips with them are fun. It is great fun to see them on our annual family beach vacations each year, being doted on by their cousins and aunts and uncles. But there are pools and waves and the chances for drowning, in my estimation, are tremendous, at least when you take into account how they compare to the chances of drowning in Manhattan.

And there's the sleeping. Am I really going to tell Addie she can't stay up late and watch a movie with her older cousins? Of course I could. But we're there to spend time and have fun, and so I don't. And as a result I end up staying up late, too, and then dealing with her crankiness—not to mention mine—the next day.

The same study found that while on vacation, those who rated their holiday as relaxed or very relaxed indicated a higher level of happiness than those who called their vacation stressful or neutral.

After the trips were over, there was no statistical significance in the difference in happiness between vacationers as compared to those who stayed home.

So if this study is to be believed and applied, the joy of vacation comes in two parts: the planning first, followed by the vacation itself *if* that vacation is relaxing.

That's a big *if* when you're traveling with kids.

It would explain, though, the jubilant social media posts of moms planning their upcoming Disney vacations. The ones I see all over Facebook—booking the FastPass, making dinner reservations months in advance, picking the perfect hotel and fireworks-watching spot—are positively brimming with joy. Because there's so much planning involved, there's also a lot of happiness.

The four of us boarded that Disney ship with nothing more planned than a dinner reservation one night for Ryan and myself. I had done some investigating of the kids clubs—Addie and Will would have to be separated because of their ages—and decided we would take advantage of them. The one Addie would attend was free and the one for Will was only a few bucks per hour.

While it wasn't exactly the lazing-away-on-the-beach vacation while I sipped cocktails and read a book as the kids played safely for hours at a time in the gentle surf with me gazing upon them lovingly, we did manage to steal a few hours of quiet here and there on a vacation that's not generally known for peace and quiet.

I have loved seeing the joy on their faces on the water slides at Sesame Place and on the Disney Cruise and seeing Addie's reaction to being transformed into Princess Anna at the Bibbiddi Bobbiddi Boutique.

But *fun* and *relaxing* are not the same thing. Not even close.

Think about it this way: If your child was grown with her or his own children, deep in the trenches of potty training and sleep training, working a full-time job and all but collapsing into bed every night after a sixteen-hour day of career and child care, what would you advise for her or him?

Maybe to take a few days away to rest and recharge?

It's not possible to give parenting your all when you have nothing left to give. It's not possible to be a good spouse when you can't even muster up the energy to ask your partner about his day. Even if a "vacation" means sending the kids to their grandparents' or cousins' house for a night or two so you can lie on the sofa with your husband for twenty-four uninterrupted hours—you'll likely be a better parent for it when they come home.

Chapter 10

Grown-Ups Need Help, Too

You Are Your Kids' Life Coach—But Who Is Yours?

" **S**elf-indulgent. Narcissistic. Too much time on your hands."

These were the initial thoughts that came to my mind when a friend mentioned to me that many people at his new company had "coaches."

"You mean like company mentors or something?" I asked.

"Yeah, we have something like that, too."

"No, like life coaches," he said. "There's one guy who has his coach come to his office every week for an hour or two. There's another senior guy who actually spends a week with his coach every few months. He flies to Texas to do it."

I literally started laughing out loud. How ridiculous, I thought. Why do people need so much help with everything? I mean just get over yourself and get on with it, I thought.

Besides, I'd been doing OK all on my own with this self-improvement stuff. It had been months since I undertook the Happiest Mommy challenge. Between my diet, my socializing, my sleep, my "look," and my relationships with my husband

and family, I was doing . . . OK. I mean, yes, I was happy. Happier. But was I happiest? If I was going to do this project, I was going to do it all the way. Maybe I'd taken this project as far as I could all by myself.

If my kids come to me with their problems (something I'm sure will happen more and more as they get older), I'm their coach, their shoulder to cry on. And while I have a wonderful support network, I have to wonder, who is *my* coach?

One of the most fascinating things about becoming a parent—and this is not at all an original thought, but one that rings so true—is that there is no one there to teach you how to do it. Yes, someone can show you how to change a baby, to give a bath, even to sleep train. But that's not really parenting. That's meeting the basic needs of a child. Parenting is something else entirely—something that's day in and day out. It's the shaping and molding of a child, through a million little words and actions, into the person you want them to be.

For me, the person I want my kids to be can be summed up in one word: *Happy*.

Of course I draw primarily on my own experiences of a happy childhood to inform my parenting. I look to my parents and follow their lessons of unconditional love and support. I read books from time to time. I am a member of several online parenting groups, which, between all the mommy wars, do from time to time offer sound pieces of advice.

But there are times—many times, even with my new Happiest Mommy guiding principles—when I get lost along the way. The insecurity is constant and, at times, overwhelming. Even with a sound support system, there are things that I'd rather just not burden my husband or parents with—for many reasons. Some things I just don't think they get. Mostly if I express something I'm worried about, they either tell me "You're being ridiculous, you're a great mom!" or they try to solve a problem they are in no way equipped to solve.

Maybe it was time to bring in a professional.

So I got to thinking about a woman I knew on the Upper East Side named Melanie Rudnick. She's a life coach, and I had interviewed her for a story I wrote for ABC News on her conscious-parenting classes. She seemed pretty happy.

I decided to turn to her for help with one aspect of my life that had been bothering me since, well, the beginning of this book (if not before): my daughter Addie's eating. Could getting some coaching of my own help me break through this stubborn issue with my kid? Maybe. But little did I know that Melanie's coaching and advice would soon help me through one of the most stressful times in my life.

It's Not Really About the French Fry

An issue that comes up again and again is Addie's eating. I've moaned about this earlier, and while my diet is spiffier than ever thanks to my eating makeover, Addie is still eating only one vegetable (carrot sticks). Well, two if you count French fries. There's little variety in her diet, and she would prefer to snack all day long than eat actual meals. All my online searching for exciting new ways to hide healthy foods in kid meals has been for naught.

I alternate between the mind-set of "I'm picking my battles and this isn't one of them" and massive guilt and feeling like an unfit parent. To this day, she has never—I mean literally never—eaten a piece of pork, red meat, or fish. Has never even tasted it but has an aversion so strong that she looks as if she will vomit when I suggest it.

I recognize that this food struggle with kids is not an uncommon one. But that doesn't change the fact that it's on my mind often and when I bring it up with Ryan or family, it's simply dismissed with a "Well, she's healthy and growing" or "She'll grow out of it" comment.

I know they're trying to help, but what I hear when they brush aside my concerns is this: it doesn't matter. And somehow, that infuriates me.

In other words, there's a whole lot of love, but not a lot in the way of tools.

At one point in my life, I might have tried a parenting coach or a nutritionist for Addie. But armed with my new philosophy of treating myself like I would treat my children, I decided to take a different tact. Addie didn't need support: I did. I decided to give Melanie a try—as a life coach for me. She didn't give me tips on how to force-feed my reluctant eater. Instead, she gave me other tools. Namely, the most important thing I learned from our short time together is that the narrative running in my head—the one that says I'm not doing enough, or that I'm not doing it well enough—is simply not accurate.

"Just because you think it doesn't mean it's true," she said.

We dove right into our first session. The very first question she asked me was "So what's been going on?" I launched into a minutes-long tangent about how I was simultaneously overwhelmed by doing too much and crippled with anxiety at the thought of not doing enough—the paradoxical anxiety at the center of every mother's life.

Talking to Melanie—four times in total—was very much like speaking to a friend who had very thought-provoking nuggets of feedback and exercises to work on between sessions.

Anxiety became a central theme of our conversations. Not the panic-attack–inducing kind, but rather the kind of anxiety when your thoughts start spiraling and that feeling in your gut gets worse and worse, and then all of a sudden you realize you've wasted an hour thinking about something that may or may not even happen. I know this type of anxiety all too well. I suspect you're familiar with it, too.

I told Melanie that with a family, career, two children—one with special needs—and another on the way, trying to squeeze in fitness, fund-raising for causes I'm passionate about, getting enough sleep while simultaneously moving and writing a book . . . and all that while trying to be an attentive wife/daughter/sister/friend, it often felt like things were just too much.

"The stakes are so high," I told her. "There's no room for error." Melanie and I talked at length about a situation recently, when I was trying to find a twos program for my Will to attend in the fall. I was filled with worry about this prospect, sending out emails, setting up tours and meetings, hoping it would somehow work out. I lost sleep, checked my email inbox obsessively for responses from program directors, and was sick at the thought he would somehow be left out.

And then each of the programs we looked into said they would be thrilled to have him, and it became up to us to decide.

"You took so much time and energy worrying. . . . Did you ever stop to wonder if the opposite might also be true?" she asked me. In other words, did I ever stop to think that every program would welcome him with open arms? No I had not.

And that was my other major takeaway from this exercise: "Write your worries down, and with each one ask if the opposite outcome could also possibly be true. And if it could be, it's time to let that worry go."

Melanie said that thoughts are a cycle. You have thoughts that make you feel crappy.

Because when you feel crappy, you are not your best self. In my case, that means not doing all the things I want to do—I spend time worrying when I should be sleeping, or exercising, or any of the other healthy behaviors I've spent this whole experiment trying to instill in myself—which, in turn, leads to the thoughts that I'm not doing enough, which makes me feel crappy. And around and around we go.

In a way, breaking out of this worry/anxiety spiral is the true key to being the Happiest Mommy I can be. Because if I can't beat this, I realize, I can never be truly happy.

One of my best conversations with Melanie took place after I had been traveling for a conference and had more time than usual to myself. Though I had planned on using some of that alone time to rest and recharge, it was actually quite an anxious time for me. Turns out the more time I have to think, the more I worry. And then I'm angry at myself for worrying.

It's that last feeling you need to start with, she said. "Once you let go of the feeling bad about feeling bad, you actually start letting go of anxiety altogether."

We discovered that one of the reasons I keep myself so

busy is so I don't have to deal with my thoughts, which are often anxiety producing. It was a revelation for me, and has actually made me feel a lot better about the frenetic schedule I keep. And while Melanie pointed out this coping behavior was OK for me, it would cease to be if I was dropping the ball in areas of my life (I'm not, unless you count pushing a few deadlines to their last possible minutes).

Now, when people ask me why I keep piling things on my plate, I have an answer: because I'm good at it. Melanie helped me see that my ability to handle a lot is actually probably one of my most admirable personality traits. Talk about a life lesson.

I kept up my sessions with Melanie, more or less on a weekly basis: thirty-minute check-ins via phone. On the "good weeks" there wasn't always a ton to discuss. On those weeks we mostly discussed my worries about not measuring up in the various aspects of my life—parenthood, being a good wife, being a good daughter, and of course my work at ABC News.

My job is a sensitive topic for me. On the one hand, I know how incredibly lucky I am to have it. But I often feel like an imposter. Like I don't belong there. I'm one of the few people in the newsroom who didn't attend an Ivy League school. There are many questions about current events that I can't answer, much to my embarrassment. I even dress differently from most of the people I work with. It's like they're all doing something more important than I am and as such, are less concerned with the frivolous things I enjoy, like manicures and high heels.

Of course, ABC News is a news organization, one of if not the most respected in the nation and the world. After working there, I can certainly see why. Even as a lifestyle journalist—in other words, not exactly an investigative or political or world events reporter—I'm held to the same standards in reporting. The general public might not realize that there are lawyers and clearances departments and standards advisors all in place to make sure the news being reported is right and is fair every single time.

It was, for me, the endgame. I never thought I would get there. I was working as the editorial director and national media spokesperson at Travelocity before I was hired. So that meant I was often called on to be a "talking head" in on-air travel segments for ABC News and other networks. So I would make the trip over to the Upper West Side studios, check in with security, get my hair and make-up done, and get a few minutes on camera, all the while wondering what it would be like to work at a place like that.

And then one day, while I was sitting in my cube at Travelocity, I got an email from the online travel editor at ABC News letting his contacts know he was leaving for a job at the Associated Press.

This, I thought, was my chance.

I campaigned relentlessly for the job. I went to interview after interview, and knocked every one out of the park. I knew I would get the job.

Which I did. At precisely the same time I found out I was pregnant with Addie.

Still, I thought, I could do it. Ryan was against me taking the job. The job at Travelocity was warm and fuzzy, friendly and flexible. In fact, the New York office had just gotten word we would all become home-based employees in a few months. I would have all the flexibility in the world to spend time with my new baby.

Nope. I decided to go for it anyway. I got my offer from ABC and, mostly out of the utmost respect for my then boss at Travelocity, I decided to share it with him rather than just outright quit. The salary was slightly more than what I was earning at Travelocity.

I shared this with my boss and was asked to wait until the next day to do anything final. I did. And the next morning I was given a promotion and a substantial 20 percent raise.

They had no interest in matching it. So with a nice raise and a fully flexible schedule to entice me, I left my dream of working at ABC News just like that. But it killed me that I did. And I never stopped wondering, *What if?*

About seven months later I got a voicemail from a familiar number. It was the person who had been my main contact at ABC during the initial round of interviews, letting me know they'd like to talk.

It turned out no one had yet been hired for the job. I accepted the job and told them I would start in a few months, after the baby was born. I took my maternity leave from Travelocity and then after three months at home with Addie, reported to work in January of 2012 not to my home office but to 47 West 66th Street.

Four years later, I'm still there. Compared to the throngs of people I have seen come and go in my time, four years feels like an eternity. Like I said, it was my endgame. I didn't have a plan after that. And of course my job has grown since I've been there—from handling only travel to taking over all of lifestyle—meaning parenting, pets, food, fashion, love, and more. I've reported on a few stories I'm extremely proud to have been the first to. I by and large enjoy being there.

I'm not sure what I would do next.

So when the opportunity to write a book came along, I was thrilled. Something related to, but in no way in conflict with, what I do at work. But one of the issues with writing a book is that it can very easily be—and is for many people—a full-time job. But I wasn't willing to give up my actual full-time job.

On the weeks I would classify as "not good weeks," Melanie the life coach and I had much more to discuss. I did a lot more talking those weeks. And one of those not-so-good weeks came, as they often do, right before the holidays, when moms have to do everything they normally have to do, but they also have to do everything else that comes along with having a "happy" holiday.

At the same time that the year was winding down, I was well into the third trimester of being pregnant with baby number three. Now I hate to blame irrational behavior on pregnancy and hormones, but in this particular case I really hope that was playing a factor, because it all ended with me screaming my head off on the corner of 1st Avenue and 82nd Street, right after Addie's Christmas concert.

A few weeks earlier, we had moved apartments. Same neighborhood and all, but moving nonetheless. The week prior—the second weekend in December—had been Will's ear tube and adenoid surgery, requiring two days off of work (after taking two days off of work just a few weeks prior to that for the failed surgery attempt). I was also put on a *Good Morning America* assignment on "mom bullies" that required an overnight in Chicago during a snowstorm. Because of a confluence of events, some personal and some work related, on the Monday morning when I lost my mind I had not been in my office for more than a week.

The day after the surgery was a Christmas party the kids had been looking forward to, and it was on the way to this party, carrying a stroller and two toddlers onto the subway, that the breakdown had its beginnings.

The next day, friends of ours from out of town were scheduled to come for a visit, and having guests would have been OK if I hadn't nearly killed myself to get the kids to the party the night before. If I hadn't been home caring for a very sick little boy the whole day prior to that. If the two days before that hadn't been spent in Boston meeting with doctors and going through a surgery, albeit minor, with a toddler. If the weeks prior to that had not been spent moving once, then closing on a house and moving again. If I didn't have a full-time job and a book to write. If the pregnancy hadn't just started to get to that uncomfortable stage when everything hurt.

But it all got done, and the breakdown, while certainly percolating, managed to be kept at bay for another thirty-six hours. Our guests left town on Sunday, and the work turned to preparing for the week ahead.

The next morning—manic Monday, as I have come to call it—was Addie's Christmas concert. I would be late to work, but the concert was in the morning, and then I would head to the office to spend the rest of the day catching up.

The parents had been given the option of taking their children out of school for the day after the concert or leaving them in for the day. I made plans with our closest parent friends in the class that we would leave our girls for the day. They'd have fun, we said. It was going to be a play day, as opposed to an academic one.

After the adorable final song, the four-year-olds' rendition of "Joy to the World," I caught up with the other parents and was told they had decided to give their daughter the option of coming home for the day, which she chose to do. So I didn't know exactly who would be left at school, but the teacher assured us it was only seven of the twenty-two kids leaving, so I knew Addie would be fine.

The trouble is that I opted to leave the group of parents standing outside for a moment as this was all unfolding to use the bathroom. And in that three minutes, Addie, who was still inside, caught wind that not everyone was staying at school and became very upset. Her teacher brought her to the door where she saw Ryan and cried that she, too, wanted to go home.

Ryan decided that Addie could stay home from school, too. The other parents, who also work, had volunteered to have Addie go with their daughter to their home with their nanny for a few hours. A few hours. Like maybe three. This, Ryan had apparently rationalized, would be enough time for me to do whatever it is I had to do for the day.

I got back to the parent group and was informed of the change of plans. By now, Addie was outside, excited to be off on a school-day adventure.

My head started spinning.

I was so stunned at the callousness with which my responsibilities were being treated and dismissed as flexible that when the other parents, their nanny, Ryan, and my own mother (who had come to the concert) started asking me questions about a plan I had literally found out about less than thirty seconds earlier, I couldn't think, let alone speak.

"So what time do you want us to keep her until?" asked the mom I'm friendly with.

"Does she have her lunch with her?" asked their nanny.

"What do you actually have to do today?" asked Ryan.

"Would it be helpful for me to get her in a few hours?" my mom asked.

Like bullets from a firing squad, the questions, which I had no answers to, were being peppered at me. I kept saying, "I don't know, I don't know, just give me a second." But see, they all had places to be, too, and no one wanted to wait, they just wanted to try to offer solutions.

I finally spit out that I would pick up Addie from her friend's nanny and then get Will. The tears were coming at the utter and complete dismissal of my plans by Ryan, who I had felt I had spent the last several days accommodating.

Plus, of course, beyond that, all the incredible stress of the last six weeks.

And as we said good-bye to Addie and her friend and her friend's nanny and started walking away, I finally lost it.

Lost. It.

What started out as a raised voice turned into full-on yelling in less than a minute. I started screaming at Ryan how he had no right to do that to me, no right to alter my work day without my consent. I started screaming at my mother for simply existing, although in retrospect, she was the only person who was trying to help me. I was in a full-blown panic attack, sweating, tears rolling down my face and pushing Will in his stroller down 1st Avenue, trying to get him to school as fast as I possibly could so I could maximize my work time.

Ryan was following me, trying to remove the stroller from my shaking hands.

"You're having a nervous breakdown," he shouted at me. And I was. I knew I was. I was shaking and crying and screaming I don't know what.

"Get away from me!" I kept screaming. "Just go to work! I'll handle it, go away!"

Ryan pried the stroller from my death grip and announced he would be taking Will to school.

I don't lose it easily. I really don't. The fuse is very, very long. I may get a little snappy here and there, but I typically only reach a full-on freak-out a few times a year, if that.

I did get to do my work that day, and I did calm down. I eventually apologized to all involved. I even managed to purchase a Starbucks gift card for the friends' nanny who was so gracious to take Addie with her with no prior notice.

That little act, though—the gift card—is exactly the kind of thing moms do that dads just . . . don't. And it was one small act, but one that felt necessary, on an otherwise crazy day. It's one little thing that moms do every single day that their husbands will never know about. One more stop. One more swipe of the credit card. One more way we attempt to keep ourselves tuned in to a polite society, to express gratitude, that our husbands just literally never think of.

It's the ordering of birthday party invitations and the thank-you notes that follow. It's the Christmas cards that require careful photo selection, addressing, and mailing.

It's the making sure there's a variety of food in the apartment so the kids aren't eating the same thing three days in a row.

It's the million little things we do every day, the things we never mention, the things that seem to go unnoticed. The things you don't even bother talking about or asking for help with because in the time it took you to explain what exactly it was that needed to be done in the manner in which you would like it to be executed, it's just easier to do it yourself.

So much feels just that—unnoticed. And it's all those "little" things (food shopping, thank-you notes, parent-teacher meetings) that have to be fit in between all the "big" things (child-rearing, career, writing books, moving) that tend to be the source of the resentment moms feel.

It seemed that resentment was the very thing that could ruin all the work I'd done up until this point to become the Happiest Mommy. Because while there are many external factors we can in fact control to make our lives better—the food we eat, the sleep we get—there are internal struggles we need to make peace with if we're ever going to be able to be truly happy. For me, that means letting go of the scorekeeping. Even with the realization that Ryan does a tremendous amount for our family, it still feels like I'm always doing more. Or at the very least, that I feel the pressure of parenthood in a more extreme way than he ever will, leading to the perception that I do more.

In any case, the scorecard was never going to be even in my mind. There would be times, months, maybe even years, when I would bear the weight of parenthood. Perhaps there will be a time in the future when it will come down more on Ryan. Maybe not. Either way, I needed to let it go, as the song says. It wasn't getting me anywhere. It was only serving to make me act like an insane person and lash out against the people I loved most.

I had a session scheduled with Melanie a few days after the manic Monday street breakdown. I relayed to her the story of what had happened. Much of what she said to me on that day didn't resonate. She talked about simply asking Ryan for more help, for making my needs known. But the truth is, Ryan is exceptionally helpful. He does ask me regularly what I need him to do to make my day easier. He often takes the kids to give me the alone time I need to accomplish the tasks I've piled on my plate.

She did make one point, though, that made a lot of sense.

Melanie pointed out that all the things I had on my plate—the career, the book, the many kids' activities, the nine therapy appointments per week I had advocated so hard for for Will and the six therapists I needed to coordinate to accomplish them, the time I carved out with Addie so she too would feel special, the house, the new apartment, the baby.

They were all choices I had made. No one else put those things on me. I did it all to myself.

Huh. That was definitely true. I had been offered several opportunities to work in lower-profile, less-stressful jobs. I had taken none of them, even those that were higher paying.

I had been thrilled at the opportunity to write a book when it came my way, and wouldn't hear of not writing it.

I had insisted that we move apartments when we found out I was pregnant with our third child.

And the baby: well, I'm so glad Ryan was on board and was so excited at the news. He is one of two, and seemed OK to leave our little family as is and leave the baby days behind. I was the one who couldn't let go, the one who needed to hold a newborn just one more time. The one who was positive all of our lives would be even better with another person to share it with.

After every session, Melanie sends me an email with a quick recap of our conversation and her advice. This is immensely helpful, because it relieves me of the burden of having to take notes during our session and remember the takeaways.

It is true that you are certainly busy, but try and remember, it's your choice to take on everything that you do. When we make a choice, we have two choices from there. You can either accept and try to enjoy whenever possible by focusing on the good stuff and realizing everything is a choice.

The other option is to resist our choices, which never feels good, and appears as stress, anger, and other negative feelings. When the negative feelings come up, it's important to think about whether or not changes need/can be made.

Take some time to think about how you would like your life to look when it comes to everything you put on your plate. Letting some stuff go could quite possibly lead to you feeling better, which allows you to show up and be more calm and present.

I was hit, suddenly, with a thought that was as sad as it was true. So many good things had happened to me in the last year and I had enjoyed so little of it. Everything was just a race from one thing to the next, with no end in sight.

It would appear that I had everything I had always wanted. Lovely new apartment. A book deal with a major publishing house. Forward career movement, with more and more regularity on *Good Morning America*, something I had been working toward since I walked in the doors at ABC News.

Most importantly: loving husband, happy kids.

This left me with one burning question: What the hell is wrong with me?

"You're the only crazy one," Melanie joked when I asked her this question. She said I have something she calls "not enough-ness" and it's one of the most common issues she sees with her clients who are also moms.

"They manifest in different ways," she said. "But it all comes from the same place, wanting to be the best mom possible." She said that the manic Monday breakdown was not at all unusual. "It's the feeling that you're doing everything, and yet you're not doing enough."

Bingo.

She reminded me about my choices to keep so busy and to remember that they were, in fact, my choices. No one was forcing me into them. Just realizing there is a choice, she said, often is enough to start feeling better.

She relayed a story about another client, one who at the

time had fifteen-month-old twins. She was at the playground with them, and hating every second. All she could think about was how she didn't want to be there.

And then, Melanie said, it occurred to the woman that she didn't actually have to be there. She could get up and walk away at any time. There was no one there to stop her.

Of course, she didn't. But just the realization that ultimately, it was, in fact, her choice to be there made the moment she was in more bearable.

How many times have we looked back on a season in our life and wished we had enjoyed it more? Melanie said for her, that was in her late twenties, when she was living in a "crappy" studio apartment in the West Village, desperate to meet someone and fall in love. Those things did happen for her, and now Melanie is married with a four-year-old daughter.

But just recently, she said, she was speaking to a twenty-something in a similar situation. Melanie told the young woman she would love to go back to her life then, the one in the crappy apartment, for just one week. "I wish I had enjoyed it more," she said to me of her life back then. "The last thing I want to do is look back on this time and feel the same way."

It's one of my biggest fears, too, and the prime motivation for writing this book. I want these years with my kids to be happy. These days and years when they care for no one outside our family. The days that are filled with busyness, but also filled with so much love and laughter. The days when they adore me.

I don't ever want to look back and wish I had enjoyed it more. I want to enjoy it in the moment.

So how do I do it? I asked Melanie.

Turns out once again, the answer lies with our children.

"You know when you ask Addie how her day was, and she says good, but that's all you can get from her?"

I did indeed. I had to be reassured by her teachers that she was happy at school and having a ball each day.

"It's because kids live in the present," Melanie said. "By the time you've picked her up at school, school's done. And she's totally focused on the next activity, the one she is involved in at that very moment."

Kids have so little past, and aren't sophisticated enough to think too far into the future. As a result, the only place they live is the present.

"It's the exact opposite of adults," she said, "who live almost exclusively in the past and in the future."

Her primary advice is to put away the phone. It is a big step, she said, to being in the present.

I'm actually not a big abuser of the phone in the first place, but I figured there's always room for improvement. So I do. And immediately, I'm happier. And the kids are happier because they have more of my attention. And then I'm even happier because they're happier.

One day, Addie has a half day. Will and I pick her up and then Addie and I drop him off at his afternoon program and head out to lunch. I leave the phone in my bag.

We talk, we laugh. I marvel at the way she engages the strangers sitting around us at Shake Shack. She tells me four-year-old jokes, which make no sense to me but that she, and therefore I, find hilarious. We share cheese fries. She orders a strawberry milk shake but then decides she prefers my lemonade and we share that, too. She tells me how happy she is to be with me and how this is the "best day ever."

That night she tells me over and over again how much she loves me.

I've stopped looking at the phone altogether when I'm having one-on-one time with the kids. I am not as important as I think I am, I remind myself, and decide to give myself permission not to respond to emails or texts other than the ones from my boss, Ryan, or my parents for twenty-four hours.

When I'm at home, I now leave the phone in the kitchen. It's a lot harder to mindlessly troll Facebook or get involved in a group text involving mostly emoticons when the phone is not on your person. I start to forget about it, for the most part.

I miss nothing. I gain so much.

Conclusion

Luke

I've gained so much by being a happier mommy. But the most important thing I gained was another child.

It was somewhere in the middle of the journey to becoming the Happiest Mommy that I became pregnant with the baby now known as Luke Ryan Brown. He was born the day after I submitted the first ten chapters of this book. He is the perfect person to complete our family.

It occurs to me that had I not taken on this experiment, it's very likely Luke might never have come to be. You see, it was all those tweaks and changes that made me incrementally happier. Because I was happier, because I was calmer, I became open to the idea of a third. And here we are.

But as babies are wont to do, little Luke—Lukiedo, as we call him—threw our lives into a complete tailspin. I had just gotten used to the juggling act of two kids, and now there were three. And if you're one of three kids, or have three kids yourself, you've probably heard more than one person tell you that the third one "practically raises himself." I was under the impression the third child would be the kind of roll-with-it child that would be superchill and easy.

Luke apparently didn't get the third-child memo. I can say without hesitation that the first three months of his life were far more difficult than the first weeks of the lives of Addie and Will. Now some of that may be Luke's personality (turns out he doesn't like to be put down, ever. Very convenient!) or it might be simply attributed to the fact that the two other children who require so much attention just weren't around the other two times we had a newborn in the house.

Around the time I found out I was pregnant with Luke, I came across a 2014 study that suggested that while a first and second child increased levels of parental happiness, the third child did not. The research, conducted by the London School of Economics and Western University, Canada, found that while "parents' happiness increases in the year before and after the birth of a first child, it then quickly decreases and returns to their 'pre-child' level of happiness.

"The pattern for second births is similar, although the increase in happiness before and around the birth is roughly half of that for first births. The increase in parental happiness surrounding the birth of a third child is negligible."

Well, I thought, that's fine for everyone else. But obviously that isn't true for us. Clearly, we'd only be happier with the arrival of our third baby!

I can sit here and say that after several months—and a good night's sleep—that is in fact the case. But the last three months? Well, they've been a shit storm.

All of my Happiest Mommy practices went promptly out the window. I was forbidden to exercise for six weeks after Luke's birth. I ate whatever was lying around or ordered takeout. Though I came home from the hospital with only a few pounds of baby weight to lose, I actually managed to gain five more after Luke's birth, so poor my eating habits became once again. Not to mention the lack of exercise.

And the sleep. My god, the sleep. There was none. Twelve Hours by Twelve Weeks Old? Luke was having none of it. But it wasn't entirely his fault. You see, I decided that I would keep this little baby with me as much as possible, including while we slept. So with every little sigh, every stir, I was awoken. But I couldn't bear to let him go. Until I went to the pediatrician for his four-month well baby visit. I described to him the disaster that was our apartment each and every night. He told me to do two things: get Luke out of our bed and put him in another room, and feed him once—once, not 4 to 5 times—overnight by waking him before I went to sleep and then letting him figure it out. That's a euphemism for cry it out.

I had boldly stated earlier in this book that if 12 by 12 didn't work, I would gladly do cry it out. But when it was time to actually do it, I got a little soft. "He's just a baby!" I thought. So I put it off.

But at the five-month well baby visit, the doc asked me again how the sleep was going. When I told him there had been little improvement, he reiterated his sleep plan and told me I wasn't doing Luke any favors by continuing down the path we were on,

I wasn't doing my marriage any favors either. Let's just say the lack of sleep led to significant . . . tension . . . in the house. When I returned to work, things only got worse. When I started dozing off in the makeup chair before an appearance on *Good Morning America*, I knew things had to change.

So I did what the doctor advised, and soon after Luke was sleeping from 7 p.m. to 5 a.m.

My favorite rule of Happiest Mommy-ing was back—sleep at any cost—and literally overnight, things began to look up. Luke—little Lukiedo—has attended his first Baby Beethoven classes and seems to enjoy it, as do I. I'm once again the outsider—the mom no other moms talk to—but that's OK now. I made so many new friends and connected with old friends that I feel content in my friendships, all because I made them a priority. And this time I have matching socks.

It took awhile to get the wheels in motion on the other rules. But speaking of motion, I did keep my promise to run the 2016 marathon and I am deep in training as I type the last words of this book. Getting back to running has done so much for my mood, and on each day I can squeeze a run in, I am a better person for it. Happier, more productive, and more peaceful.

And it seems to be rubbing off on Addie, too. She routinely asks to join me on a run, and every so often we lace up our sneakers together and hit the park for a few sprints suitable for a four-year-old. If we can keep it up, she'll grow up to be not only an expert in toilet-paper usage but a lover of running, too.

One of the most dramatic changes I've seen—and never saw coming—is how quickly those mom friends came to be such an important part of my life. Yes, my college and childhood friends will always be a huge part of my life. But these women—perhaps because of our similar life circumstances, perhaps because of the close physical proximity of living in the same neighbhorhood, or perhaps because they are just really wonderful people—have grown to be a tremendous source of joy for me. They've helped me out in a pinch with the kids time and time again. They've included us in parties and playdates galore. They've been so kind to my children. They've brought gifts and came to visit when Luke was born. They've made motherhood even more fun.

As far as the vacations go—well, I took a page from the book of that mommy blogger and did leave Luke home from a vacation when he was about twelve weeks old. But I didn't steal away with Ryan. Instead, we took Addie and Will to Disney World, and they had the time of their lives. And yes, I did manage to do about a day's worth of work while I was there. Some habits die hard. That vacation with Ryan though? It's happening in a few weeks. Hotel booked, plane tickets purchased. We'll be gone for a week, and I can't wait.

As for Ryan, he continues to amaze me with his love for our family. Watching him with the kids is such a joy. When I stopped looking to criticize and started looking to praise, there was so much wonderful to see.

I've learned so much about myself over the course of the

Happiest Mommy project. The golden rule of it—treat yourself as you would treat your kids—is the core. But there's also been a realization that happiness isn't something that happens to you. It isn't a result of the luck, or money, or really anything outside of our control. It's a choice.

Addie is four now, and headed to kindergarten soon. Will is off to pre-K at the same school. Luke just turned six months old. The tears come each time I realize how fast time goes by. For today, for now, I'm still the center of their worlds. I don't know how much longer it will last. But in the meantime, for as long as it does, I choose happy.

Acknowledgments

The idea for this book originated as a segment on *Good Morning America* about an experiment I conducted called The Baby Diet. I was sitting at my desk when one of the show's senior producers, Alberto Orso, called me to see about shooting a piece based on an article I had written. That phone call eventually led to this book, and to you, Alberto, I am forever grateful.

Which leads me to my agent, David Doerrer. Thank you, David, for being home sick that day and watching *GMA*. Thank you for reaching out to me to encourage me to expand the idea of the diet into a book. Thank you for seeing me through several rounds of proposals and for holding my hand through publication. Thank you, thank you.

To Michelle Howry, for your support, encouragement, and insightful edits, thank you. I am so grateful for all the ways you made this book better. To Meredith Vilarello, for seeing this through to publication, thank you. It couldn't have been done without your dedication.

To my own mother: Even after 200 plus pages of book, I lack the appropriate words to thank you. Your love and support enables me to lead this wonderful life I live. You have made having it all possible for me. I will never be the person you are, but I promise I will always try. Dad, thank you for giving me your love of words, writing, and books. You are my hero.

Of course, I must thank my children. Without you, this book would not have been possible. Without you, happiness is not possible. You are the light of my life, and I consider myself the luckiest person in the world to be your mother. I did nothing to deserve you, but I am so eternally thankful that God chose you to be mine.

And, finally, to my husband and best friend, Ryan. You have supported me every step of the way in writing this book. Thank you for being on this crazy journey of life with me. I could not ask for more. I love you more than you'll ever know.